Bearii

'Thanks to this superb translation by Nick Caistor and Faye Williams, English-language readers finally have access to Mercedes Núñez Targa's crucial evidence about the appalling cruelty inflicted on women during the Francoist repression. *Bearing Witness* is a classic work of prison literature that has played a major role in keeping alive the memory of the crimes of Franco.'

—Paul Preston, historian and author of *Architects of Terror: Paranoia, Conspiracy and Anti-Semitism in Franco's Spain*

'Mercedes Núñez Targa belonged to a young antifascist generation which fought Franco and his Nazi backers in the war of 1936–39 in Spain. Imprisoned, but eluding the obliteration Franco visited on so many, she escaped to fight with the resistance in France, and was deported to the Nazi camps. This first ever English translation of her humane, vivid and painfully honest testimony of incarceration under two fascist systems flares up for readers today an urgent signal in our own moment, of clear and present danger.'

—Helen Graham, Professor Emeritus of Modern European History, Royal Holloway

Bearing Witness

Prison Stories from a Woman's Fight Against Fascism

Mercedes Núñez Targa

Foreword by Pete Ayrton
Introduction by Mirta Núñez Díaz-Balart
Translated by Nick Caistor and Faye Williams

First Published in Spanish in 2016 by Editorial Renacimiento, Seville, as *El Valor de la Memoria*
English language edition first published 2024 by Pluto Press
New Wing, Somerset House, Strand, London WC2R 1LA
and Pluto Press, Inc.
1930 Village Center Circle, 3-834, Las Vegas, NV 89134

Originally published as two separate books:
Cárcel de Ventas was originally published in 1967 in Spanish by Éditions de la Librairie du Globe, colección Ebro, París
El carretó dels gossos. Una catalana a Ravensbrück was originally published in 1980 in Catalan by Edicions 62, Barcelona
These works are translated into English as 'Ventas Prison Madrid' and 'Destined for the Crematorium' in this English language edition.

www.plutobooks.com

This book has been selected to receive financial assistance from English PEN's PEN Translates programme, supported by Arts Council England. English PEN exists to promote literature and our understanding of it, to uphold writers' freedoms around the world, to campaign against the persecution and imprisonment of writers for stating their views, and to promote the friendly co-operation of writers and the free exchange of ideas.
www.englishpen.org.

British Library Cataloguing in Publication Data
A catalogue record for this book is available from the British Library

ISBN 978 0 7453 4908 4 Paperback
ISBN 978 0 7453 4910 7 PDF
ISBN 978 0 7453 4909 1 EPUB

This book is printed on paper suitable for recycling and made from fully managed and sustained forest sources. Logging, pulping and manufacturing processes are expected to conform to the environmental standards of the country of origin.

Typeset by Stanford DTP Services, Northampton, England

Simultaneously printed in the United Kingdom and United States of America

Contents

Foreword

Pete Ayrton

A permanent revolutionary for whom politics was an essential part of her daily life, Mercedes Núñez Targa lived through and was active in major events of the twentieth century: the Spanish Civil War, World War Two, the Nazi Concentration camps. She influenced Spanish politics when she was alive, and her books continue to influence Spanish politics after her death.

From Franco's death in 1975 and the transition to democracy, Spain has been divided between those who argue that it is best to not rock the boat and let bygones be bygones and those who want perpetrators of Franco's brutal rule to be brought to trial, statues of leading supporters of the regime to be removed, and streets commemorating Franco's supporters to be renamed. As part of this process, in 2019, Franco's remains were removed from the basilica of the Valley of the Fallen, a national monument, and taken to a cemetery in Madrid where his family has a private vault.

Since its end in 1939, 85 years ago, there has been a constant effort by progressive forces to remember just how brutal the Civil War was and for the memory of the defeated to be celebrated. This initially occurred in a context where many democrats advocated that the transition to democracy would be best served by concentrating on the future. The 1975 Pact of Forgetting made sure that there were no prosecutions for human rights violations or similar crimes committed by Franco and his supporters. The pact was given legal basis in the 1977 Amnesty law. However, advances in DNA technology have made possible the identification of the remains of those executed by Franco's supporters. Since 2000, the Association for the Recovery of Historical Memory has led a campaign to identify the many 'disappeared' during the War. In 2007, the Socialist government passed the Historical Memory Law which recognized war victims on both sides and formally condemned the repressions of the Franco regime. In 2020, the government allocated €400,000 for the opening of mass graves and the exhumation of victims of execution. More recently, in 2022, the government of Pedro Sánchez passed the Democratic Memory Law which makes the government take full responsibility for exhuming and identifying the bodies of those killed by the Fascist regime.

Literature is also a contested terrain for this struggle; there are many in the literary world who believe that arguments over the Civil War have for too long held back Spanish literature. They argue that what is needed is to recognise that crimes were committed on both sides and move on. *Bearing Witness*, the first part of which was published in 1967 by a Spanish Communist party publisher in exile in Paris, goes against such an attempt to forget and move on. It reminds us clearly of the brutality of the Spanish and German prison guards and how, at the end of the war, Nazis and Fascists remained in positions of power and authority. Its author, Mercedes Núñez Targa, is in no doubt that the crimes of those who ruled with such cruelty should be punished in the most severe way possible – but not at the cost of the victims losing their sense of dignity.

Giving witness after the end of the war at the trial in Carcassonne of René Bach, the French interpreter for the Gestapo, Mercedes Núñez Targa insists on keeping her humanity and not being brought down to the level of her captors:

> I leave on the verge of collapse. But I walk out with my head held high. No, Nazism has not defeated me, it has not made me employ its own methods. Because in the duel between the torturer and the tortured, it is the torturer who, inevitably and without remedy, forever loses their own dignity.

Bearing Witness is not only about the inhumanity of the prison authorities, it is also about the many daily acts of resistance among the prisoners. Indeed, an outstanding quality of Mercedes Núñez Targa's account is her ability to find hope and resilience in the most brutal of environments. The women in the camps put aside differences of nationality and class in creating the solidarity that enabled them to resist the brutalities of the camp authorities.

In the HASAG camp near Leipzig, the women are given the task to recover a large quantity of glasses from a bombed factory. They organize a chain to bring out the glasses:

Suddenly, someone trips and drops a box, with a loud crash of breaking glass. Everyone bursts out laughing. It's like a signal. We break all the glasses, ruthlessly... we emerge from the basement euphoric, smiling at each other, terribly proud of our first sabotage.

Emboldened by this success, Mercedes Núñez Targa knows what to do when set to work on lathes cleaning shells.

She is told repeatedly how to do the job. A supervisor 'comes over and sits on a box. He points to my red triangle with no letter on it and asks me my nationality.

"Spanish."

The man looks at me, startled.

"*Spanisches? Franco oder Pasionaria?*"

"Pasionaria.'"

She quickly learns how to impede the functioning of the machines. She perfects her technique of sabotage: the results are more and more dramatic:

The shells are getting increasingly catastrophic and I'm ecstatic, when suddenly there is an extraordinary crack, a shell whistles out and the entire machine shakes with noise as if it were the end of the world; the shaft has broken.

I'll admit it: I freeze. I hadn't meant to go so far. Sabotage of this kind can mean hanging or a trip to the gas chambers.

The *obermeister* rushes over. He barks in such a way that I can see all his gold teeth and even down his throat.

'Sabotage! Sabotage!' he bellows...

In one of the extraordinary moments of *Bearing Witness*, the blonde supervisor defends Mercedes telling the obermeister that it can't be sabotage since the woman does not understand a word of German and could not understand how the work had to be done.

It is the same supervisor who knew that she was a Spanish political prisoner who identified with the left-wing leader, La Pasionaria.

Throughout her amazing life, Mercedes Núñez Targa enjoyed such moments of good luck as well as bad. At no time did she lose her commitment to radical political struggle. It is excellent that we now have her book in English at a time when the struggle against reaction can be inspired by the brave steadfastness of Spanish republicans like her.

Pete Ayrton
January 2024

Introduction

Mirta Núñez Díaz-Balart

VENTAS PRISON MADRID

In this book, Mercedes Núñez Targa creates a model of testimonial literature. The pages of her memoir describe the journey of survival undertaken by those defeated at the terrible conclusion of the Spanish Civil War. The underground voice of Ventas prison extends from the days of the legitimate Republic to clandestine life under the triumphant Fascist regime after 1939. A literature denouncing terror, the horror of the executions, and the farce of the collective trials in which the rebels judged those who remained faithful to the government. *Cárcel de Ventas* was first published in 1967 in Parisian exile by the Ebro publishing house, run by the Spanish Communist party, who took the risk of publishing this diary from Franco's Spain, something unthinkable at the time within the country itself.

In fact, when the memoir came out in France, nothing like it existed in Spain. The names of the political prisoners featured among its pages were a path opening the possibility of recuperating their lives and their deaths. Among those who suffered the first blows of the Franco regime against the defeated were the 6,000 women held in the main women's prison in Madrid, crowded into corridors after being sent back to the capital in cattle trucks from concentration camps and jails all over the country.

Mercedes Núñez, her memories still fresh when she wrote this book, recovered the survivors' voices. She was the first to highlight the stories of women such as Matilde Revaque,[1] Matilde Landa (whom she loses contact with when Matilde is transferred to the Palma de Mallorca prison), Julia Lázaro or María del Rey. She introduces us to remarkable prisoners united against torture and their fight for dignity in the most terrible conditions. They

xi

won't be the only or the last: Rosita Ventura and Dolores Cuevas, who shared Mercedes' misfortunes, ended up in front of a firing squad. But she introduces the reader not only to those shot: there were others who suffered torture, went mad, or lost their children on this arduous path.

All these pariahs were accompanied by an array of martyrs, including the Thirteen Roses, or Matilde Landa, their deaths punctuating daily life in Ventas or the other prisons they were transferred to. The ex-prisoner Tomasa Cuevas also waved a banner against the Francoist repression from inside Spain, publishing *Mujeres de las cárceles franquistas* (*Women of Franco's Prisons*) Madrid, Casa de Campo, 1979, at a moment when so many seemed determined to forget, in the name of vague pacts made in the Transition. Tomasa travelled by train to visit her former cell-mates who were trying to live quiet lives, but opened up to her about their struggles to survive those terrible years.

The presence of children only served to increase the punishment of their mothers, and made the survival of the young ones almost a miracle. As Juana Doña recalled in her precursory novel-testimony, when she was transferred from Alicante to Madrid a soldier asked her what was in the railway wagons, and she answered: 'dead children and shit'.[2] Thousands of women were unable to survive the rigours of these transfers, and for those who survived they only added to their weakness from hunger and the filthy conditions they suffered in prison. In Mercedes' memoir, the vile case of the young boy known as 'Lenin', or the madwoman cradling a tin plate as a remembrance of her child's death remind the reader yet again of the pitiless way infancy and maternity were crushed. In response to these children's deaths, a female gaoler spits: 'One less Red seed'.

Mercedes Núñez's memoir outlines the prison odyssey of political prisoners in the immediate post-war years. Thousands of women were imprisoned thanks to a twisted interpretation of *legality* whose aim was to punish and make suffer those who had not supported the military coup and hence the military victory it led to.

How was it possible that in the regulation 'inquiries' where the inmate was taken to testify:

they take you out of the prison and give you a good beating, or use electric shocks, or do whatever they like with you. And you come back a few days or weeks later, in pieces... or you don't come back at all. (p. 8)

Routine physical torture was doled out constantly, in even the most extraordinary circumstances. Two young girls who had not yet been tried denounced the fact that 'they beat us in front of the judge himself' (p. 43). Nor does youth prevent extremely long sentences being handed down. On one occasion, the inmates congratulate a companion for being sentenced to *only* twenty years and a day.

Describing the atrocities provides no crumbs of comfort. From the mother weeping for her daughter killed by an epidemic, to the inmate who declares 'washing in here is a luxury'. The lack of water is like a thread running through the misery of the prison. In the section on *The Young Ones*, where Mercedes denounces the presence in Ventas of a fifteen-year-old girl sentenced to thirty years (p. 14) we see how many different kinds of people were caught in the prison net.

Mercedes' accusing finger points to the *cour des miracles* of Ventas prison, where 6,000 women (and sometimes as many as 9,000) are crowded into corridors and cells. The range of inmates she describes could not be more varied. The '*dykes*', that is, the lesbians, are closely described: they are the allies of the prison authorities, who want them to 'entice' the political prisoners so that they will become part of the huge array of '*wicked degenerates*' that the new regime has created, with the intention of converting the defeated into criminals.

Time and again, we see that age is no defence against repression, not even for death sentences: 'Aren't they ashamed of condemning a white-haired woman to death?' (p. 14) The wing for women over sixty, who in those days seemed very old, demonstrates how they are deemed guilty simply for being mothers or daughters of men linked to the Popular Front, or with sons in the Republican army.

The author also writes of new kinds of relationships, like the inmate who adopts a woman badly affected by her son's execution.

She now calls her 'my prison daughter'. Others, such as Atanasia Alguacil, work in the prison workshop where there are 'a handful of girls who every night go to give her a kiss, as if she was their mother' (p. 55). Atanasia was shot by firing squad on 9 October 1941 in the Cementerio del Este.

As the sentences are handed down, Mercedes describes the *modus operandi* inside the prison, from the presence of the judges to how death sentences and reprieves are communicated. This terror following the fall of Madrid reveals that at first, the women sentenced to death were not held separately, but were spread throughout the prison in their lamentable state. In one instance, a hundred condemned women are taken out into the prison yard and made to line up. A priest slowly reads out the names of those offered a reprieve. Only nine of the hundred. A similar number is taken to the Salesas Palace of Justice to face an emergency military tribunal, with only one defence lawyer, whom they have not met until only a few minutes earlier. The first accused 'faces a deluge of questions. But no sooner has he begun a response that demolishes the arguments of the accusation than a stentorian "Be quiet!" cuts him short' (p. 40).

After being sentenced to death, the unfortunate women end up in:

> ...a tiny basement, without light or ventilation. They have not been allowed to leave it, and so have been unable to see the rest of us. In the basement itself, a small altar was set up, so that they would spend what was left of their lives meditating on the afterlife and 'becoming reconciled with God'. (p. 57)

The rhythm of executions is unpredictable. Sometimes it is a gale of suffering that sweeps away dozens of condemned women in a short space of time; at others there is a strange pause. This uncertainty, together with the rare reprieves, makes it possible to avoid mass uprisings in the prisons. It also allows room for lies and deceit. When Dolores Cuevas is being taken out to be shot in the middle of the night, the prison governor appears, and tells her and Atanasia and the other condemned women: 'you're being called to the judges'.

From her cell comes Atanasia's voice:

Why do you want me to think the judge wants to see me? I know you're taking me to the firing squad. It wasn't enough for you to execute my son. The Torrejón Fascists are going to be celebrating tonight! (p. 58)

The prisoners are constantly being coerced, and reading about it is almost unbearable, as in the case of a baby still breastfeeding who is left to cry with hunger in order to try to force his mother, who has been condemned to death, to confess before she is sent to face the firing squad. When she remains steadfast in her Communist faith rather than the Catholic one, the baby is taken away. Mercedes tells us she was taken to the La Inclusa foundling home, adding one more to the long list of lost children. There are countless attempts to coerce the inmates. To one inmate working in the workshop, the nun supervising the room says: 'If you work hard in the workshop, you won't be transferred' (p. 55).

Moments of joy are few and far between, but there are a handful of times when there is a glimmer of hope. One first of May a rose is smuggled in inside the package that 'Peque's' mother gives her. The entrance of the USSR in the Second World War is celebrated with a shout of 'We shall crush them!'. Constantly subjected to humiliation and merciless attempts to tame them, this promise of victory lends the inmates some hope.

Mercedes' escape from Spain after her years in prison can be explained by a simple bureaucratic error and is in no way far-fetched. The 280,000 prisoners of the immediate post-war years, the vast majority of them political prisoners, are a difficult number to control by even the harshest of totalitarian regimes. The use of makeshift jails that turned Spain into an immense mousetrap of repression failed to prevent the existence of nooks and crannies offering unsuspected hiding places and possibilities of escape.

These pages of faithful memory reveal what the Francoist victory meant in everyday life. A victory that contained no generosity, but on the contrary vicious reprisals against the defeated and their kin. It is not easy to take in the details and remain unmoved. Mercedes Núñez Targa is a witness for all those women who did not live to tell their stories. Thanks to her we are able to recover their individual and collective suffering and hope.

DESTINED FOR THE CREMATORIUM

In these pages, Mercedes Núñez Targa has written a fundamental chapter in Spanish testimonial literature. It is also a moral fable about human behaviour in extreme situations such as her stay in a Nazi concentration camp, Ravensbrück. *Destined for the Crematorium* is a dramatic portrayal of atrocities, and yet at the same time of the solidarity of the oppressed that transcends frontiers, genders, or nationality. In such dreadful circumstances, the bonds of family and friends, the fraternity of shared ideas, and moral awareness are the mainstay of collective existence when the enemy is trying to reduce the prisoners to the state of animals. Mercedes' response in her testimony is to turn the oppressors into feral beasts who fight one another and verbally abuse prisoners who from the very first moment have been weakened physically and mentally. As she writes:

> The SS officers, male and female alike, fight over the prisoners' clothing, jewellery, furs, purses; behaving like animals, guffawing as they shamelessly scoff the contents of the torn Red Cross parcels we had so ostentatiously been given. (p. 83)

There are two Mercedes here: her as an individual, and as part of the collective. The first Mercedes comes from a bourgeois family, and studied what was then seen as necessary for a young woman to make a good marriage. Mercedes separates herself from her background and becomes part of the collective world of the fight for social and political change. She joins what nowadays we would call an environmental movement, the Amics del Sol (Friends of the Sun), an association that encouraged working class youngsters to come into contact with nature while at the same time encouraging fraternal co-existence between the sexes. This was the new woman being born under the Second Republic, a woman who knows the importance of economic independence and paid employment. Mercedes's next step was to join the JSU (Unified Socialist Youth) which attracted so many young people who were drawn to the Left to fight national and international fascism. This was a political trajectory that was far from exceptional in the middle class from which she came, which was one of the main bases of support for Republicanism and the Popular Front.

Mercedes Núñez Targa's life was that of a passionate but not blind militant. Mercedes was deeply committed to all the struggles for emancipation in the 1920s and 1930s, dedicating herself to them with the enthusiasm of a charismatic young woman. Her political party involvement was born of the July 1936 military rebellion. The urgent need for anti-fascist unity against the rebellion led her from the JSU to the Spanish Communist party.

How did this Communist militant who had fled Francoist jails succeed in reaching France, only to end up in a women's Nazi concentration camp? The answer lies in Mercedes' involvement in the anti-Nazi struggle of the French Guerrillas, and her capture in the rearguard in Carcassonne, where her house is 'used by Guerrilla command and serves as a safehouse when necessary'. (p. 66)

Hundreds of women accompanied her to Ravensbrück, where 'around 250 women were deported because of their participation in acts of resistance on French territory'.[3]

One of her companions in misfortune, Neus Catalá, who also survived the camp, and went on to write about her experiences, tells of her arrival at Ravensbrück: 'we made our triumphal entrance to the world of the dead at 22 degrees below zero on 3 February 1944, among a thousand women, to be received by the SS with their machine-guns and dogs'.[4] The site one sees on film today, with swans swimming on ponds, the landscape dotted with trees, gives no hint of the evil some human beings had unleashed in such a beautiful spot.

One of the most interesting aspects of Mercedes Núñez's account is her literary construction of human beings who are thrown together and find themselves united in the concentration camp. Mercedes does not present individuals who are monolithic in their evil, or heroes sculpted in granite in the anti-Nazi struggle. She offers us men and women, with all their weaknesses and strengths, who yield or resist, depending on the stuff they are made of.

When the concentration camp was liberated in 1945, she returned to her starting point in France, Carcassonne. Still there were the guard dogs and the SS who ruled the roost with their whips and pistols, humiliating and barking insults at their prisoners. Bach, the man who caused Mercedes Núñez so much pain and physical torment, was brought before the judge. But this woman who was destined for the crematorium sets aside the possibility of revenge. Bach's physical appearance and mental collapse brings out the compassion that still exists in the heart of a cruelly mistreated woman:

> Not the conceited Bach, he of the white jacket and perfumed handkerchief, but a defeated man, dressed in a dark convict uniform, dirty, scruffy, unshaven, looking at me with the eyes of a cornered beast. And suddenly it's as if a bucket of cold water has been thrown over me. How could I lash out at an enemy in chains? (p. 146)

The book contains many instances where the victim achieves a moral victory by not stooping to reprisals against the recently defeated and their collaborators. In this way Mercedes Núñez underlines how faithfulness to a set of ideals can mould human nature. At the same time, she criticises those who have not fought against Nazism but volunteered to work in Germany, and now insult pitiful German women: 'The real disgrace is that these women... who have voluntarily served Hitler, feel they can insult them. And your soldiers, instead of attacking defenceless women and children would do better to go after all the Nazis walking free in Germany.' (p. 142)

Mercedes juxtaposes the small, everyday acts of heroism with what is going on in her mind, depicting the duality of the human condition and how hard it is to overcome this: 'I have been hungry and have even thought of stealing food from a fellow prisoner' (p. 65). A risky fraternal action – warning a camp inmate that wearing glasses would lead straight to the gas chamber, is immediately accompanied by a typical rebuke: 'I don't dare tell her I berated myself for having done so' (p. 130).

This desire to tell the truth is plain from the very beginning of her memoir:

> it isn't about creating a literary work, it's about telling the truth. And that I can do. It riles me when people portray themselves in their memoirs as perfect heroes, who were never afraid, never thought of filling their bellies, the pure spirits! (p. 65)

The journey undertaken by Mercedes Núñez dissipates the cloud of heroism surrounding other biographies and instead offers us the human clay of those who feel passions they succeed in overcoming. This arises not only from a desire to be different from their gaolers, but also because they have seen the moral destruction of those companions who did not manage to withstand the torture of the Nazis and their hunting dogs. Nazi ignominy is contrasted with the solidarity of those fighting for freedom, in these beautiful words: 'There is nothing in the world stronger than the sisterhood of those who fight together' (p. 69).

The itinerary of horror leading the resistance fighter in France to the camp is similar to that experienced as a prisoner in Spain. They are led to degrading filth, to uncertainty about their future, to the hunger that is another sort of pain, and to torture. The mistreatment comes in various guises. From crude torture to: 'shouting and pushing, they usher us out, without even letting us put our clothes back on' (p. 85).

Mercedes outlines the survival strategies employed when faced with a torturer determined to reduce his prisoner to the level of an animal. René Bach, the incarnation of evil, appears well-dressed, clean and sweet-smelling, in contrast to the beaten prisoner:

> You find yourself facing him after five or six days in a cell, with no means of washing yourself; dirty, creased, ragged. Then, when Bach lays eyes on you he makes a face, as if to say 'Ugh, how disgusting!', doesn't say a word – which is more humiliating than any beating – and sweeps a white, very white, scented handkerchief under his nose. (p. 72).

How well here Mercedes shows how being physically clean can represent both a pure desire, as with the prisoners, or can conceal inner vileness as is the case with Bach. The study of how to face this and other torture is the expression of the combat between power and submission, two people locked in a struggle, one trying to crush and create a terrible, uncontrollable fear; the other attempting to change the destiny awaiting them:

> (Bach) Young, intelligent, quite the psychologist, a genius when it comes to interrogations, he plans his sinister work like a chess player moving a piece, not thinking of this move but three or four moves ahead. He asks a few trivial, insignificant questions, and suddenly *bam!* the trap they hadn't seen coming, backing his victim into a corner. Off with their heads! (p. 73)

In response, the resistance fighters employ two strategies: talk or keep quiet. 'To tell him a story is too risky. It's best to keep quiet and face him in silence. To give the arrested resistance fighters their due, almost all of them chose the second strategy.' (p. 73)

They had to avoid being defeated by pain or indignity. The situation of those who had been crushed demonstrated the reason not to give in:

> Bach manages to morally destroy him. Gripped by fear, sweating anxiously, hands trembling, Mari blabs, telling all, making up what he doesn't know, sinking deeper and deeper, losing every shred of human dignity. And Bach, observing his handiwork, has a glare of contempt in his eyes that makes my blood boil. (p. 73)

When the time for revenge comes, Mercedes rises above it, and does not make the Nazi murderer pay with an eye for an eye: 'No, Nazism has not defeated me, it has not made me employ its own methods.' (p. 147)

This memoir is not a tale of victims and atrocities; it is above all the story of the fight for personal and collective dignity. The devastating effects of Nazi power are cleverly undermined by the concentration camp women. They are not alone in fighting against the wish to destroy them. The moment of oppression is also that of solidarity not only between the prisoners but also an underground solidarity that surfaces in the German workers themselves when they connive in the sabotage of production. The response is also in that stirring collective rendition of the anthem of the French revolution: 'Never again have I heard a *Marseillaise* quite like it. Nobody has ever sung the hymn of the *"sans-culottes"* with more strength and conviction than we did in that coal-mining city.' (p. 87)

Mercedes Núñez Targa's account of the horrors of Fascist oppression ends with a confession of the difficulties she finds in returning to normal life:

I have to overcome the fear of going back to normal life, re-learn, like a little girl, simple things like paying rent, going to the bakery to buy bread, saying hello to a neighbour; to get out of the moral ghetto, the 'I'm no longer like the rest of them', 'those who haven't been in the camps will never understand us'. (p. 147)

Doubtless what they have lived through does somehow make them different. And the path that clears the way to a return to normality is an arduous one.

Mirta Núñez Díaz-Balart

NOTES

1. See Mirta Núñez Diaz-Balart and Antonio Rojas Friend, *Consejo de guerra: los fusilamientos en el Madrid de la posguerra, 1939–1945*, Madrid: Compañía Literaria, 1997.
2. Juana Doña, *Desde la noche y la niebla (mujeres en las cárceles franquistas, Madrid, de la Torre*, Madrid: Ediciones de la Torre, 1978, p. 72.
3. Rosa Torán, 'Ravensbrück, el campo de las mujeres', in Ángel del Río (ed.) *Memoria de las cenizas: Andaluces en los campos de concentración nazis*, Seville: Aconcagua, Junta de Andalucía, 2013, p. 57.
4. Neus Catalá, *De la Resistencia y la deportación*. Barcelona: Adgena, 1984, p. 86.

PART I

Ventas Prison Madrid

A practising Catholic born into a well-to-do family, I did not appear in any way predestined to follow the path that was to become mine.

Like all young people in Spain during the 1930s, I passionately followed the events of those years and all the political turmoil. I was a supporter of the Republic, but this never translated into concrete action. Until the very last minute, I smiled in disbelief whenever anyone mentioned the possibility that an uprising was imminent. How could the Right rebel against the Republic after the February 1936 elections, when Spain had chosen the Popular Front? It was absurd.

But what I thought was absurd soon became a reality. The first gunfire in the streets of my city put paid to my peaceful existence. I could no longer remain neutral. Together with many thousands of youngsters of my generation, in a few hours I went from being a passive spectator to active participation on the side of the Republic.

Although sincere and enthusiastic, that participation was extremely modest and completely anonymous. I didn't fire a single shot or make any speeches; my name didn't appear at the foot of any article; I didn't become a heroine of production. And yet the Franco regime did me the great honour of considering me sufficiently dangerous to incarcerate me for several years, and a tribunal in all seriousness judged and sentenced me for 'aiding the rebellion' despite what they described as my 'excellent record'.

'Explain to the people outside what you have seen in here'. Those words, said by an inmate of Ventas prison as she hugged me goodbye, have nagged away at my conscience like an unfulfilled promise. It wasn't until twenty years later, as best I could, that I set down this necessarily incomplete story. Perhaps Clara wasn't called Clara. Perhaps I attribute to Rosita a sentence spoken by María or Luisa. I can't be certain. My main concern has been to recreate as faithfully as possible that crazy period after the end of the Civil War as experienced by the women in Ventas prison. To you, young people, 'children of the victors and the defeated', I dedicate this book with admiration and affection.

'VENTAS PRISON, THAT MARVELLOUS HOTEL...'

The bolt on the outside of the cell door slides back and a Falange[1] official appears, in her navy-blue cloak.

'To the judge,' she announces drily. 'Follow me.'

At the end of the solitary confinement wing, I step out into the extraordinary world that is Ventas prison in this Year of Our Lord 1940. A staggering number of women – pale, with hunger etched on their faces, some dressed in scraps of fabric from blankets and mattresses – are crammed into the corridors, staircases, even in the latrines. Everywhere is strewn with dozens of rolled-up sleeping mats, suitcases, earthenware jugs, cloth bags, tin plates...

The women crowd together to watch me go past. There are furtive smiles, friendly gestures, and one young woman even raises a clenched fist behind the official's back. Each and every friendly act is like a ray of sunshine to me after the endless silence of the punishment cell.

It's over with. After a brief, intimidating interview with the judge – a young officer with an effeminate air – my solitary confinement has been lifted.

The prisoners rush to meet me, hug me, ask me questions:

'Where are you from?'

'When were you arrested?'

'Have they knocked you about much?'

'What have they got on you?'

Ángela, a woman from El Escorial, who on more than one occasion had risked being caught and punished for venturing as far as my cell, takes me by the arm authoritatively.

'You're coming to my corridor. I've talked to the "trusty" in charge and the girls and even though we're already chock-full, we'll squeeze up a bit more to make room for you.'

(Later on I came to fully appreciate the significance of this gesture of solidarity in Ventas prison, designed to hold 500 prisoners but now containing more than 6,000, where every centimetre of space is precious).

In the corridor, the prisoners surround me, vying with each other to offer words of advice:

'Be careful who you talk to. There's a fifth column in here too.'

With Ángela's help, I manage to install my sleeping mat; rolled up it serves as a chair, and I settle myself down on it. From this vantage point I glance curiously around me. None of the prisoners sit idle. The women's nimble fingers are busy crafting intricate keepsakes.

When I ask, lots of them show me the exquisite objects they have fashioned from the most unexpected materials and with infinite patience: little lace cloths, embroidered aprons, artificial flowers made with electrical wire and silk threads, espadrilles in the shape of butterflies, little donkeys made with scraps of blankets, complete with reins and saddlebags.

'That's nothing,' says one woman, noticing my admiring glances. 'You should see what the menfolk make! Show her the sewing basket your boyfriend made you,' she says to a young blonde girl.

They all start pulling out things made in the men's prisons at Porlier, Torrijos, Yeserías…

'You should see the beautiful box that a woman in the corridor on the left was given by her husband. He's facing "Pepa" in Porlier,' says a lively brunette.

'"Pepa"? What do you mean?'

'What? You don't know?! Pepa means the death penalty. They've even made up a song about the men sentenced to death in Porlier. Listen.'

And with the grace of a true Madrileña, she intones a pure chotis:[2]

> Pepa, you should see the girl,
> She has half of Madrid in a whirl,
> She's taken quite a shine to the commies…

'Don't sing that, my girl,' an old woman reproaches her. 'It's no laughing matter.'

'I know, grandma. But the condemned men themselves have set the example. Singing when they know they're going to die shows that even if they send half of Madrid to the firing squad, they won't see them tremble.'

'That's right,' says another girl. 'We sing to get on their nerves. Nothing would make them happier than to see us crying into our beds all the blessed day!'

And they all sing together:

> *Madrid jail is a great prison,*
> *It really must be said.*
> *Where the prisoners, through lack of care*
> *Are simply left for dead...*

After that come countless other songs, full of rebelliousness and unexpected good humour. The recital culminates in the Ventas song to the tune of 'La Madelón',[3] sung by the whole corridor at the tops of their voices:

> *'Ventas prison, that marvellous hotel...'*

Ending with:

> *For now he lives the high life,*
> *But we're plotting his demise.*
> *Franco will be crushed,*
> *And the people of Madrid shall rise!*

At this, a female guard rushes into the corridor, screaming hysterically:

'Shut up! I'll put you all in solitary!'

'That's the mad queen,' one of the women tells me derisively.

THE ROLL CALL

A guard appears. Her bony face is framed by a grey mop of hair, as stiff as wire and with a fringe down over her eyes. Her enormous feet appear to be shod in a pair of flat shoes.

'That's "Cristóbal Colón" (Christopher Columbus),' some charitable soul whispers.

The nickname is so funny (and may the illustrious discoverer of the Americas forgive me) that I struggle not to burst out laughing.

'Girls, line up! Girls, roll call!' shouts the 'trusty', to no great effect.

Finally, by hook or by crook, they get us to line up in pairs. 'Cristóbal Colón' counts and recounts us, gets muddled up, and in the end settles for accepting the number the 'trusty' gives her.

Arms raised, we are forced, as every day, to sing the sickening Nationalist anthem 'Cara al Sol'.[4] The prisoners are so slow and so obviously unenthusiastic that we have to put up with singing the Carlist Oriamendi anthem as well.[5]

'*For God, the fatherland, and the king...*'

But when we reach a certain verse, I notice there's a delightful variant that the author of the Carlist anthem didn't envisage:

> *Whatever the cost*
> *We have to make sure*
> *Spain sees the return*
> *Of the government of Negrín...*[6]

'Cristóbal Colón', who is at the far end of the corridor, wheels round in a fury. She doesn't know what to do, and so decides to yell the ritual slogan:[7]

'Spain!'

'One!' we answer feebly.

'Spain!'

'Great!' – Three or four repeat it.

'Spain!'

In a powerful outburst, we all shout defiantly:

'FREE!'

RATS

Night falls. The inmates start to unroll their sleeping mats. Arguments break out:

'You've "eaten" my square.'

'Who, me? Just count: one, two, three.'

'Look here. No more than two and a half.'

'Move your mat a bit. I've no room for my bed.'

'Nor have I.'

After lengthy discussions everyone manages to find a place. Ángela and the companion to my right, a young, very pale girl, teach me the extremely delicate art of laying out a mat in the reduced space of three squares by seven, that is, sixty centimetres across and one metre forty long.

'This is the time of day I always remember my kids,' Ángela tells me. 'Every night I used to kiss them when they went to bed, and now, poor things…'

She rummages in a cloth bag and takes out a small photo.

'This is my eldest, see? Maybe my father will bring him the next time he visits.'

'And your husband?'

'In France.'

'Mine too,' says the pallid young girl. And in a faint voice, she adds:

'I had a girl as bright as the sun. Newly born when I was arrested. She died on me in here, last year. There was a terrible epidemic and, with no water, no hygiene and a complete lack of care, the children died like flies. Six or seven every day, sometimes more. Since they didn't know what to do with them until they were buried, they piled up their little bodies in a latrine. The rats would come to eat them, and so to prevent that, we mothers stood guard. I spent the night scaring the rats off because I didn't want them to bite her…'

FIRING SQUADS IN THE CEMENTERIO DEL ESTE

I wake with a start and see all the women sitting up on their mats in expectant silence. It's still night. Lips are trembling, eyes are clouded over, fists clenched.

'What's going on?'

'Be quiet!'

What are they listening to? However hard I try, all I can hear is the sinister howling of dogs in the distance. They're howling at death… A spine-chilling sensation leaves me breathless. Could it be…?

Now comes the growing noise of an engine. It must be a lorry. Drawing closer. It passes in front of the prison, then gradually fades away. All of a sudden, the noise ceases: the lorry must have come to a stop. The dogs' howling becomes more intense, piercing, almost human, then unexpectedly also ceases. There's a deathly silence and a wave of violent emotion seems to sweep along the corridor. Ángela covers her ears. An old woman prays quietly. Several women are crying silently.

'Ratatat!' the unmistakable rattle of a machine gun tears through the silence. And with it, all along the corridor arises a chorus of shouts, sobs, furious curses:

'Murderers!'

'Swines!'

'Mother of God, how long must this go on?'

'Children of my soul!'

'Silence!' shouts a harsh voice.

Everybody tries to hold their breath. Almost immediately we hear short, separated gunshots: the *coups de grâce*.

'Three, four, five, six,' Ángela counts under her breath.

Eighteen.

Eighteen Spanish men have just been executed in the nearby Cementerio del Este.

That's how the women in Ventas prison wake up every morning.

INQUIRIES

A guard appears, calling out a name:

'That's me,' one woman replies. 'What is it?'

'To inquiries,' the guard replies in a quiet, almost contrite voice.

'Mother of God!' murmurs the woman, the colour draining from her face. She raises her hands to her chest.

'Swines!' Ángela mutters angrily.

'What does "inquiries" mean?'

'Inquiries? Well, to get you to blab they take you out of the prison and give you a good beating, or use electric shocks, or do whatever they like with you. And you come back a few days or weeks later, in pieces… or you don't come back at all.'

'But that's illegal!'

'My girl, you've no idea what Fascism is like. What do they care about legality! Nicolasa Blas Santamaría, from the third on the right was set free. Some freedom! At the door to the prison some Falange bigwigs were waiting with a car. They took her to a Falange office and gave her a good thrashing. Seven madmen hitting her! Result: Nico, who was as sturdy as an oak, came back blind on a stretcher. Her sight came back bit by bit, though never completely, but she has never been able to straighten up again, and at the age of twenty-six she is as bent over as an old woman. Every so often she gets fits of madness and has to be restrained, because she doesn't recognise her companions and thinks she's still in the hands of the Falange. "Cowards!" she shouts. "It takes seven of you to beat up a woman!" And there are so many like Nico, not counting the ones who left for "inquiries" and never came back…'

The woman who is to be taken out for inquiries dresses clumsily, helped by two other inmates. She murmurs:

'My children, my poor children…'

Spontaneously, all the other women bring her something from their scarce reserves: a tiny slice of bread, a tomato, a piece of salt fish.

A guard comes in, shrieking:

'Where's the woman wanted for inquiries?'

'Here,' replies the woman, and her voice is firm. Surprised, I study her. She is still very pale but raises her head and looks steadily at the Falange official.

As she is leaving the corridor, she turns to us and raises her hand in a brief gesture:

'Here's to you, comrades,' she says simply, without raising her voice.

'She won't talk,' a girl declares.

WATER

'What I'd give for a good bath!' I announce.

'Wouldn't we all!'

'Washing in here is a luxury.'

'When you see the queue for water, you'll faint.'

Two girls approach me.

'Look, the two of us have a bucket and we both wash in the same water. If you want, all three of us can share it.'

'They're very clean girls,' Ángela backs them up, handing me a tiny bit of soap that she keeps like a hidden treasure.

So the three of us wash in the same bucket. To do so there's nothing for it but to exhibit our sad, malnourished prisoners' bodies to the whole corridor, which scandalises a few old crones.

Once we've finished, I prepare to throw the dirty water away. The other two stop me.

'Wait. We can use it to scrub under the mats.'

Which we do. Then we go to pour the water away in the latrine – it's a big empty cooking oil drum: there's no water in the latrine either, and any inmate using it has to pour some of the dirty water from the drum to flush it. This one latrine is for the entire corridor – around two hundred women – as well as the sick women in the infirmary, the 'fímicas' as consumptives are known here. There's a long, permanent queue.

'It's a miracle we don't catch typhus,' says one of the girls.

The two of us take our bucket to the yard where there's a trickle of water from a tap. Around it there's an extraordinary, noisy queue of hundreds of women carrying cans, buckets or jugs.

'There are water pipes all over the prison,' the girl tells me in answer to my questions. 'There are even showers, washbasins, baths, and sinks. That's because it was built during the Republic. But "those people" have shut off the water and left only that tap. For 6,000 women. And in 1939, there were 9,000 of us! On the one hand, they want to force us to live in filth, to lower our morale, make us suffer. But above all they want to pit us against one another for a glass of water.'

As though to confirm what she's saying, a violent argument breaks out next to me:

'Hey you, join the queue!'

'Who, me? I've been here over an hour. I'm before you.'

'That's not true. I saw you arrive.'

'Me?'

9

'Yes, you. Who let you in?'

'A woman who left.'

'Join the queue!'

All the women join in a heated discussion. Finally, despite her vehement protests, the woman is forced to go to the back of the queue.

The slightest attempt to 'push in' is met with a vociferous 'join the queue' that forces the person to comply.

Next to me, a good-looking woman is explaining:

'In my village, Colmenar de Oreja, half the inhabitants are in prison. And there are tons of death sentences... Hey, that woman in blue is trying to push in!' she suddenly shouts, breaking off her story.

'As I was saying,' she continues after a while, 'in Colmenar de Oreja what happened was that at the start of the war... Hey, you with the jug, get in the queue!' she yells once more.

We all laugh. I don't think I'll ever find out what happened in Colmenar.

A COMMUNIST LEADER

All of a sudden, a woman, still young, pale and serious-looking crosses the yard with a bucket in her hand. She heads straight for the tap without anyone (a miracle!) protesting, and equally calmly places her bucket under the stream of water.

'Aren't you going to say anything to her?' I ask the woman from Colmenar jokingly.

'She's been sentenced to death,' she replies gravely. 'Here in Ventas the ones facing a firing squad don't have to queue.'

The pale woman, her bucket filled, passes by us. In the friendly greetings the women offer her there is both affection and respect.

'She's a communist leader. Matilde Landa. A real woman, intelligent and brave. Just imagine, one of her relatives who's a big shot in the regime came to offer her a reprieve and even her freedom if she publicly renounced her ideas. She replied that she's a communist and prefers a thousand times to die before selling out.'

'You should see how much the condemned women owe her,' the woman from Colmenar adds. 'She takes it upon herself to give them advice and to sort out all the paperwork. And there's more. Before, there was a time when any member of the Falange could come, without any authorisation from the judge or anything, take away a woman and have her shot on his own account. Thanks to her, that's been put a stop to. Utterly fearless, she went to confront the governor and gave him what's what, and as a result ever since he doesn't dare allow anyone to be "taken out" without an execution order. That woman is worth her weight in gold.'

THE MADWOMAN

One of the prisoners in solitary is Eugenia, a Catalan woman. Eugenia is mad. The presence here of this poor madwoman is utterly irresponsible, in itself a terrible accusation against the regime that has locked her up.

Eugenia is a woman of indefinable age, tall, skeleton thin, hair cropped short. All she ever has on is a coarse, filthy nightgown that due to her height barely covers her knees. She walks round day and night carrying a tin dish. She eats, washes – on rare occasions – and urinates in this dish. At night, she swaddles it carefully, cradles it like a child, and puts it in her bed.

When we pay her a visit through the bars on the corridor, she greets us with incoherent phrases:

'I love you very much. Tonight, I'll go in the train.'

This morning, Ángela and I went to visit her.

Eugenia receives us with her eternal mad smile, dish in hand.

'Last night I saw them,' she moans. 'There were five of them.'

'I've heard you're from Barcelona,' I say to her in Catalan. 'What street did you live on?'

Hearing her mother tongue, Eugenia seems to be transformed. In her lifeless eyes, there's a sudden flash of reason. Overcome with emotion, she seizes my hands until they hurt and gabbles in Catalan in a hoarse voice filled with such raw pain it makes me shudder:

'My daughter! My daughter! They killed her right before my eyes.'

She starts panting. Suddenly, as if deprived of all her strength, she lets go of me and leans against the bars of her cell, drooling.

Slowly all conscious expression drains from her face. She peers all round her as if in search of something, and smiles sorrowfully when she finds her dish, which had fallen to the ground. Ignoring us, she turns her back, raises her dirty nightgown and starts furiously scratching her scrawny buttocks.

Shocked, we look at one another. What dreadful circumstances can have driven this poor woman mad?

'LENIN'

A discussion is swirling round us.

'I think it's true that they killed her daughter. "Those people" are capable of anything,' Rosita insists. (Rosita is the young woman who says we should sing 'to get on their nerves').

'I'm not sure,' another woman says doubtfully. 'The poor thing isn't in her right mind, she can say anything...'

'What about Lola Bernal? Is she mad too? And you know what they did to her boy.'

'Oh, be quiet, for heaven's sake, don't remind me!'

'What happened to Lola Bernal?' I want to know.

The women look at each other, grim-faced. It's Ángela who eventually breaks the silence:

'When Lola was arrested, they gave her such a dreadful beating that ever since she constantly spits blood and spends the whole time in the infirmary. Then, when the police grew tired of beating her, they brought in her son, a little boy no more than two years old, and started fooling around with him. The poor little angel answered them in baby talk and was laughing innocently.

'What's your name, sonny?'

'Lenin,' replied the boy.

(Of course, the little fellow had a different name, Miguel or Luis or whatever, but everybody called him 'Lenin').

When they heard this, the police became like wild animals.

'"So your name is Lenin? Well then, take this, Lenin!"

Right there in front of his own mother they picked him up by the legs and started smashing his head against the wall time and again, until they left him for dead.'

'How is that possible?'

'His mother is here in Ventas, and she's not mad like poor Eugenia. Go and ask her.'

'They've got the hearts of wolves,' a peasant woman says slowly.

ELOÍNA

'I don't know whether it's true about Eugenia's daughter or not and I don't know if we'll ever get at the truth. But one thing is very clear: in no civilised country can a mad person be held responsible for their actions, and they cannot be locked up. That's against all the principles of justice,' I say.

'What do you mean, justice? Don't you realise, my girl, that we're living under Fascism? In Spain today not a soul says anything but "I'm doing this because I want to, and that's all there is to it", replies Inés, a spirited, dark-haired woman. Do you know the story of Eloína?'

'No.'

'Well Eloína was a poor, half-witted woman who did no one any harm and was the laughing stock of all the young kids on the streets of Madrid. When the war broke out, somewhere or other she found a priest's cassock, put it on, and went round proudly wearing it, in the same way as if she had put on a dancer's dress or a minister's hat. That was in 1939, and she was sentenced to death. Of course, you didn't have to be very smart to see at once that the poor woman had, as they say, a screw loose... but the tribunal refused to see it.'

'Was she killed?'

'You bet! Back then the condemned women weren't kept apart during the night the way they are now but were in with the rest of us. The night they "took out" Eloína was horrible. The poor wretch, when she saw them coming in the middle of the night brandishing their pistols and shouting her name, she began to scream in terror; she tried to hide among the sleeping mats, clung on to us begging us to save her, wanted to hide in a toilet...'

When finally they succeeded in hunting her down, she yelled, cried, refused to walk. They dragged her along the floor as if she was a sack. Several of the other women collapsed with nervous fits. I don't know how we didn't all go mad that night!'

THE YOUNG ONES

A noisy group of young women crowds round a young girl who arrives from Las Salesas.[8] I go over as well.

'What did they give you?'

'Twenty years and a day.'

'You lucky so and so!'

The joyful cries of the JSU (United Socialist Youth)[9] when they hear her sentence leaves me stunned. I was expecting them to sympathise with her!

'I came out all right,' the girl says simply. 'But Antonia is facing the 'Pepa'.

'What swines they are!' screams a girl. 'Aren't they ashamed of condemning a white-haired woman to death?'

'Yes, it's true she has white hair,' replies the newcomer, 'but she also has guts, and could teach us youngsters a thing or two. "I'm communist", she said, as proud as proud can be, "and as secretary general of the communist party in my village I accept responsibility for everything my party has done." And when one of the judges tried to say she had stolen and looted, she shut him up at once, telling him "Communists don't steal!" He was left speechless. I'm telling you, the only thing she didn't do was sing the Internationale...!'

'What about you?'

The girl smiles.

'I tried to leave the JSU looking good.'

'If anyone ever told me that one day I would see a girl being congratulated on being sentenced to twenty years in prison, I'd have thought I had lost my mind,' I tell the small group of JSU women.

They all laugh heartily.

'The important thing is that you're not taken to the cemetery. As for being sentenced for years, huh, the more they give you, the more they'll owe you,' one of them says.

'How many years do you have?'

'In age, fifteen. In prison, thirty,' she replies cheerily.

The look of astonishment on my face makes them all laugh.

Suddenly there's a strange silence. Following their gaze, I notice a small, ugly-looking girl who is passing by, glancing furtively at us.

'There she goes.'

'A curse on her.'

The girls' comments are full of hate and disgust.

'Just look! She's wearing the JSU shirt,' I say quietly, surprised at this.

'Ha! If you or I were to wear that shirt, the same night we'd be in the punishment cell and find ourselves charged with "incitement to rebellion" and end up in the cemetery. But she can get away with anything. Because, however inoffensive she looks, she's a stool pigeon who must have tens of deaths on her conscience. She's called – remember the name – Carmen Vives Samaniego. She was the one responsible for the thirteen young girls being executed.'

THE THIRTEEN ROSES

They were thirteen young girls from the JSU as bright as the sun. Blanquita, the youngest, was not yet sixteen. As soon as the rebels entered Madrid, the girls organised themselves and, risking their lives every day, they dedicated themselves to finding refuge for a lot of too well-known anti-Franco people who were in great danger. But that rat came and told them she would introduce them to some comrades who were also organised, etc. Instead, she set a trap for them and when the girls arrived there, they found themselves face to face with the police.

The girls were sent for trial to Las Salesas – Vives together with them – and were condemned to death, while Vives got twenty years. When they got back here, you can imagine how horrified everybody was: they were waiting for them with their hearts in their mouths. But the thirteen were not dismayed; they were still smiling.

'We've been sentenced to death,' they said, 'and the sentence is to be carried out within 48 hours. We don't care, and we're not sorry about anything. With or without us, our cause will triumph. But we want you to know that during the trial it was discovered we were arrested because of that stool pigeon,' they said, pointing at her, 'and that she herself admitted it to the tribunal to try to escape punishment.'

'You can imagine the row that broke out. Vives collapsed and the guards rescued her from us and put her in the infirmary. If they hadn't, I'm sure we would have lynched her that evening.'

'That day, 5 August 1939, was an unforgettable day for everyone in here. Smiling and as calm as could be, the thirteen young girls kept up our spirits. They washed from head to toe and put on their best rags to face the firing squad. They asked an inmate who is a professional hairdresser to comb their hair nicely. "We want to go looking good," they told her. As she was combing one of them, her hands began to shake uncontrollably, and the girl said: "Don't tremble, woman, we're the ones going and we're not trembling." What gems they were! They were like roses. When "they" came to take the girls out, they marched to their deaths like true heroines, cheering and singing. María Teresa, that Falangist wild beast, volunteered to go to the Cementerio del Este to give them the *coup de grâce*.

As for the stool pigeon, nobody in the prison will talk to her. Every so often she is taken out for a few days and then we know what's going to happen: shortly afterwards a group of young women will be brought in, arrested on charges of "conspiracy", and when we ask, they always say they fell into the trap after talking to that Vives...'

FIFTH COLUMN

'So the police came and thumped me so I would tell them where D... was. I played dumb. If you only knew, I kept thinking, that just yesterday I was talking to him...'

'Aha... So what you didn't spill to the pigs you're going to say out loud here, just like that, you silly goose,' an inmate interrupts her brutally.

The new arrival blushes, upset at the rebuke.

'A bit of respect, if you don't mind!'

'It's for your own good, my girl,' Ángela intervenes calmly. 'Here in Ventas, you need to keep your tongue zipped because there's a fifth column.'

'Well, people like Vives,' I say. 'But cases like her must be few and far between, aren't they?'

'Don't be so sure. And don't think everybody in here is on the level. There are always Falangists in Ventas – yes, my dear, Falangists, and more than a few, planted among us to sniff out all our conversations. Sometimes we can uncover them: the inmates have an extraordinary nose for that. But at others, it's hard to spot them. That's how a good woman who has been as brave as a lion and hasn't said a thing however much she was beaten, opens her mouth in confidence in here, and then is in for a surprise.'

'Also mixed in with us,' she went on, 'there are lowlifes, thieves, prostitutes and other scum. Above all there are the "dykes", who are hand in glove with the authorities. There's even one of them who is famous: "Juanita la Torero" who stands in the corridors cat-calling the girls like a man. She goes around with some of the guards who are of the same persuasion. They put them here on purpose, to see if we take the bait and they make wicked degenerates out of us, because they know that's the best way to get us to give up the fight. But they never get anywhere.'

'Besides,' she goes on, 'they're achieving exactly the opposite of what they want. Because when it's a matter of unmasking someone from the fifth column, or hissing at a "dyke", that means an end to the rows between socialists and communists and anarchists and others; it means we're all political prisoners, joined together like the fingers on a hand.'

THE GRANDMOTHERS

'If you want to wash your clothes, come with me,' says Rosita, picking up a bucket, 'but first, let's pay a visit to the old ladies.'

The wing for the old women, where most of the inmates aged over sixty are housed, is on the ground floor of the prison. A throng of grandmothers, most of them from the countryside, are crammed into the cells and corridor. Why are they here? Many of them because they had a son in the Republican army. Others because they voted for the Popular Front or demonstrated their support for the Republic in some way or other. A good many are caretakers from Madrid (because the Francoists seem to have it in for them, regarding them as responsible for everything that went on in their buildings during the Civil War: there's even a special court for them). Others simply, as Rosita says, know 'nothing at all' and don't understand about politics. A grudge, a personal quarrel with somebody who is now a Falangist, has brought them here. There is even an eighty-three-year-old peasant woman who was denounced by her own son because she had refused to hand over her land to him while still alive.

When Rosita calls out, a tall, lean old woman appears, dressed entirely in black with full skirts and apron, her hair in a plaited bun: the very picture of a Castilian woman.

'Let me have your dirty laundry, mother,' says Rosita, giving her a hug. 'I'm doing a wash.'

Without a word, the old woman brings her some clothes wrapped in a checked shawl.

'Any news about Pedro?'

Rosita sighs. Pedro is her fiancé.

'Not a thing. Letters from France aren't getting through. Or maybe he's found another girl...,' she says, trying to make a joke of it.

'God forbid!' sighs the old lady.

'I didn't know your mother was here,' I say to Rosita as we move on.

She comes to a halt, and for once turns serious.

'She's not my mother. My mother died when I was little. That grandma isn't a relative. I met her here, in the prison. She had a son – her only son – he was in Porlier prison and was shot by firing squad. When he was killed, the poor old woman lost her mind. She didn't speak or eat or anything. So I became her prison daughter and I look after her as much as I can. She loves me as if I was family. There are lots of young women here who have a prison mother. What would these poor old women do without us?'

ONE LESS RED SEED

'I'm going to the mothers, are you coming?' suggests Ángela.

After lots of twists and turns and a real obstacle course over mats, suitcases and inmates' belongings, we arrive at another wing.

As we reach it, we're hit by the choking sour stench of urine and excrement that makes you nauseous: this is the wing for women with young children.

'They're not given any soap,' Ángela explains. 'And as there isn't any water either, they have to dry the nappies without washing them. So between that and the lack of food, you can imagine how the children are. Almost all of them die.'

Sitting on mats or directly on the floor are a lot of young women, surrounded by a swarm of children. Pale-looking and skinny, many of them covered in sores. These children, all of them under five, spend all day and night locked up, hungry, frightened of the guards, witnessing people being 'taken out', hearing the firing squads at dawn; you can see all this in their gaze. There's an expression in their eyes that hurts.

Called by Ángela, a young woman appears:

'How is your boy?'

'Bad, very bad.' The woman lowers her eyes and her face displays a boundless despair. 'He's going to die on me, Ángela, he's going to die on me!'

'No, my love,' Ángela chides her affectionately. 'We mothers always get frightened.'

'If only I were outside, for heaven's sake. But what can I do in here? He's going to die on me,' she insists.

Slowly, our hearts in our mouths, we return to our own corridor.

'Do you know what "Veneno" (Venom) says whenever a child dies in here?' Ángela says bitterly. '"One less Red seed."'

A MODERN INQUISITION

It isn't hard to find an inmate in Ventas who has been mistreated and tortured: what is hard is to discover one who has managed to escape without ever suffering the routine beatings.

Beating and electric shocks are the two commonest kinds of torture. Usually these are designed to make the victim 'sing', to try to oblige them to denounce other anti-Francoists. Often though, the torture is simply gratuitous, the expression of a fierce hatred and a sadism bordering on madness.

A few examples:

I've been talking to Elena Cuartero. Elena, who is over fifty, goes round the prison painfully leaning on a chair she pushes in front of her because she no longer has the crutches she needs. With every step she takes, her face tenses with pain, and she bites her lips so as not to cry out. Her spine has been shattered in three places. An anarchist, Elena Cuartero has been sentenced to death.

'Several policemen beat me until they grew tired,' she explains. 'Destroyed by the beatings, they forced me to climb up a stepladder to clean a skylight. When I was at the top, they pulled it away. You can see the result. The police claimed I had tried to kill myself. I know they're going to kill me, that not even divine intervention can save me now, but I want the whole world to know what they have done to me.'

Nieves C. is on another wing. They cut her vulva in several places with a small razor, then sprinkled vinegar and salt on the wounds. They forced her to run naked, punching her, shouting obscenities and laughing when they saw her keeping her legs as far apart as possible.

'You look like a frog,' they mocked her.

They forced a grandmother of over seventy to ride a bicycle. The poor old woman kept falling off, covering herself with bruises. The torment continued until her arm was broken.

Maruja G. was beaten repeatedly to get her to tell them where her husband, a prominent anti-fascist, was hiding. Fed up with beating her without getting anywhere, they doused her with petrol and her on fire. Horrified, one of the policemen threw a jacket over her, saving her life, but her body, hands and neck are a mass of shapeless lumps. Her breasts are unrecognisable. 'If I have a child one day,' she tells me sorrowfully, 'I won't be able to breastfeed it'. Maruja is twenty-three.

Above all, they have taken it out on pregnant women. Many have been beaten so badly they aborted. 'You can give birth through your mouth', they shouted at one heavily pregnant young woman as they kicked her again and again in the belly. This woman, Carmen P, lost her baby, and ever since has had dreadful abdominal pains.

As far as electric shocks are concerned: on the wrists, the fingers – 'we're going to give you a bracelet and rings', the victims are usually told – on the genitals or nipples, together with a bucketful of water to increase the effect of the current; they are so frequent it would be impossible to name all the cases.

TRANSFERS

The news has travelled round the prison like wildfire: there's to be a transfer.

Women from the corridor go in search of news, and little by little the details emerge:

'They're going to Zaragoza.'

'"Ojos de Huevo" (Egg-Eyes) and Don Modesto are in the infirmary. They've approved Amancia Serrano's transfer.'

This news leaves me dumbfounded.

'Amancia Serrano? The one who was coughing up blood the day before yesterday?'

'The very same. Why are you so surprised? Not long ago those two quacks approved the transfer of a woman in labour.'

Really, nothing should come as a surprise to me in here.

'They're calling out the list.'

'I'll be on it for sure,' Ángela says with a sigh.

Rosita tries to make light of it, but nobody joins in. It's not the moment.

For the inmates who have already been tried and sentenced, transfer to a distant prison is like a sword of Damocles constantly hanging over their heads. Given the lack of resources their families have, being transferred means no longer seeing their loved ones for many months, even years. For those who are mothers, it means being deprived of the meagre comfort of avidly seeing their children through two thick iron bars, between which, like a lion in a cage, a guard paces up and down, ears pricked for the conversations.

'Here they come,' a voice announces.

'Listen!'

There's absolute silence. The entire corridor holds its breath.

It's a long list. Rosita is going. So too is Inés. Also the two girls who share their only bucket with me. And my pale neighbour, who watched over the body of her little girl in a rat-infested latrine. Ángela is on the list too.

'Damnit!' she says quietly. 'Tomorrow morning my father is coming with my eldest. To think what it must have cost them to scrape together the few pesetas for the journey…'

'Perhaps they'll arrive in time to see you.'

'No. We'll be taken down to the chapel straightaway. And from there to the train. And we won't be allowed to write or say goodbye to anyone.'

Consternation reigns in the corridor, but all the women try hard to hold back their tears. There are sisters who will be separated; mothers who have to go, leaving their daughter in Ventas; close friendships that have been forged in here that will be brutally interrupted. And yet the women remain resolute and in good spirits. Some even smile and try to pretend it's not important. They put on a brave face.

Helped by those of us remaining in the prison, the women being transferred frantically dress, roll up their mats, stuff all their possessions in their cloth bags. The guards are already pushing them towards the chapel.

Another bombshell arrives to increase the confusion.

'The corridors are no longer to be used. All the inmates will be locked in the wings. And the Buen Pastor nuns are coming to run the prison.'

The crush at the entrance to the chapel is unbelievable. The entire prison has come to say goodbye to the women leaving. The guards jostle us and yell:

'Hey, that's enough slobbering. Get back to your wings, all of you!'

Supported by another inmate, the very young, very pale Amancia Serrano moves along, a brave smile on her lips.

Standing silent and immobile by the stairs is Rosita's old 'prison mother'. From inside the chapel, Rosita waves affectionately to her, and her laughing face betrays fleeting emotion. All of a sudden, a young girl goes over to the old woman and tenderly puts an arm round her, as if taking possession of her. Relieved, Rosita smiles.

'If ever you go to El Escorial, come and see me,' says Ángela.

'I will.'

We give each other a big hug. Ángela clasps my hands.

'The people will triumph,' she says, her voice firm and vibrant.

CLARA

As announced, the same day as the transfers, the main corridors were cleared, and now we are all crammed into the different wings. I find myself in one of the typical three by three metre cells, which I have to share with another seven women. We can't even move. And at night laying out our mats is a real jigsaw puzzle. The last one to make their bed – and in this case that's me, because I was the last to enter the cell – has to extend their mat in the open doorway, with their head in the cell and feet in the corridor. But since some of the inmates also 'live' in the corridor, and because space is so limited there as well, protests abound:

'Hey, you with the feet, get them inside!'

Add to this that my cell companions are obliged to step over my mat to get out during the night, and also the fact that this door harbours unimaginable numbers of lice, and you can see that everything combines to give one a sleepless night.

If that were all! I miss the noisy bustle of the main corridor, the constant coming and going of different people: the always cheerful Rosita, lively Inés, and Ángela, my first friend here, someone so kind-hearted, so noble.

It's impossible to stay inside the cell. For two days, I have only gone inside to quickly pick up my rations and to sleep. On the third day, as I'm getting ready to go out, Clara, a woman with white hair who's a communist, fixes me with her piercing eyes:

'Skipping out again?'

I shrug my shoulders.

'I have to pass the time somehow'.

'Shall we have a chat?' she says, gesturing for me to join her on her mat.

'How do you want to use the time you're in prison?' she asks bluntly straight off.

Her question catches me unawares. I don't know what to say.

'What do you want me to do in here?'

'Precisely: prison isn't a parenthesis in life. It's a new battleground. Sterile dreams on your mat, looking back with melancholically, complaining about what might have been. None of that will get you anywhere.'

Her stern, perceptive words somehow create a profound sense of joy in me.

'They try to create in here every possible means to turn us into brutes,' she goes on. 'But against all the odds we women have to do everything humanly possible not to allow ourselves to become brutes, and to keep a sharp eye on ourselves down to the smallest detail. Any relaxation in our language, our cleanliness, however small, is very important. It means a concession to the enemy, if you follow me,' she says with a friendly smile.

'That's right: resist.'

'Exactly. So if you agree, let's go and take a look at the school,' she concludes firmly. 'But first, please roll up your mat a bit better. That's also part of "resistance".'

We both burst out laughing.

I'm in good hands.

THE SCHOOL

From the very first days and in a spontaneous fashion, the inmates who had been schoolteachers created small groups of basic education and general culture around them. In cells and corridors, women who couldn't read or wanted to further their education gathered round their improvised teachers.

These lessons grew so big that the teachers understood it was absolutely indispensable to coordinate them and to have a proper classroom. After lengthy efforts and not without difficulty, they finally succeeded in having the old assembly hall – now a chapel – handed over to them for several hours a day for schooling. So there, without textbooks, desks or blackboard, writing laboriously on any slate they could find and getting hold of pencils and paper thanks to their own scanty means, the Ventas inmates struggle to acquire learning. They are so keen to study that the results obtained are truly extraordinary. One girl who entered prison hardly able to do division is now about to sit her exams. Another one, who was totally illiterate, can now write correctly and has moved on to a group with classes of general knowledge.

Some of those, like Clara, who began as students, have begun to teach reading and writing to the ones who don't know how to.

'One of my students,' Clara tells me, 'yesterday, wrote the first letter in her life to her son, who's in Porlier prison. When she finished, she burst into tears of joy; and the others aren't far behind.'

There are many young women among the students, but you can also see quite a lot of white-haired inmates. I'm surprised to see a few of those condemned to death among them. How can it be? These women, who go to bed never knowing if this will be their last night on earth, are coming to school! My amazement knows no bounds when among them I notice Elena Cuartero, with that eternal look of suffering on her face and the way she has of constantly biting her lips to avoid crying out:

'What are you doing here?'

She gazes at me in silence for a moment before replying, as though she can read my mind:

'I come to learn to read,' she says simply. 'If I'm killed, I won't have lost anything. And if I live, I'll have another weapon against the enemy...'

That same day, I enrol in the school.

MATILDE REVAQUE

As we go up for roll call, Clara and I line up together at the entrance to our wing. Opposite us, a beautiful woman with an intelligent face and hair as black as sloes, done up in a very Castilian-looking bun, is smiling disdainfully at the official's useless attempts to count us.

'You don't even know how to count,' she suddenly says out loud.

'You do it then.'

'But I'm a prisoner.'

There is so much dignity and courage in her voice that I immediately take to her.

Back in the cell, they explain to me:

'That's Matilde Revaque. A socialist. She was governor of Alacuás prison during the Republic. A lot of the Ventas guards served under her. She's been condemned to death.'

'Do you remember?' one girl says, 'when Millán Astray came to see her?[10] Pilar Millán Astray,' she explains, 'it was her, along with many others, who denounced her. She was imprisoned during the

Republic in the prison Matilde was in charge of. So one day she came here to goad Matilde, who had already been sentenced to death. She began saying vengefully that she was glad to see her 'in the same conditions' as she had been in. Matilde silenced her coldly:

'No, not in the same conditions. You were on your own in a cell, you had a bed, a table, a chair and decent food. I share my cell with all these companions, sleep on the floor and am given disgusting rations. And yet,' she went on, 'all that is perfectly logical. The Republic was a humane regime and treated its prisoners humanely. Francoism is the complete opposite...'

'And so on. Some woman! The other one squeaked like a rat. The fact is, if she had come hoping to see Matilde tremble, she was disappointed. As they say, she put her in her place right enough.'

'MY COMMISSAR'

Clara, 'my commissar', is a curious woman. What boundless energy she has in that tiny, broken body of hers. She's often to be seen leaving the cell, clean and tidy, to walk round the prison. Whenever she sees an inmate sitting sadly on her mat, downcast and listless, she heads straight for her. Very determined, she submits her to a brief interrogation:

'Can you read and write?'

It doesn't matter if the woman answers: 'a little', 'a lot', or 'not at all'. If she only knows a little, Clara declares straight off:

'Come to the school. You'll learn more there.'

If she knows a lot, the implacable 'commissar', in a voice that brooks no argument, tells her there's a shortage of teachers in the school. And if she can't read or write, she simply asks her name.

'Tomorrow without fail, to the school. If you don't come down, I'll be here to fetch you.'

If she's in a wing and sees an inmate with the hem of her dress unstitched, or if it's torn under the arm, Clara comes to a halt in front of her.

'Sew that up.'

'Oh, what's the point, in prison?' the other woman replies, shrugging her shoulders.

Clara's voice becomes stern:

'That's fine! So we comrades around you don't deserve any respect? And you yourself, woman?'

Sometimes the person in question is a bit upset or ashamed, and tries to excuse herself:

'I don't have any thread...'

So then, out of a bag she always has with her, a triumphant Clara takes a whole array of threads, needles and even a thimble.

'Here, sew it up right now. Or I can do it, if you prefer.'

Usually no one can resist her. She may be too rigid, too much of a busybody, excessively authoritarian. Her total self-confidence and self-control make her someone who is slightly dehumanised, inspiring respect, esteem, complete trust, but rarely affection.

Sometimes I contemplate her when she's asleep. There, free from her stoical carapace, I can see her as she really is: a woman, no longer young, tired, in poor health, who must suffer just like the rest of us and sometimes feel the overwhelming desire to confide her troubles to someone, to lean on a friendly arm. Whenever I see her like that, vulnerable and touching, I tell myself I will say something affectionate to her, invite her to confide in me; but the next morning when she appears, so energetic and inaccessible once again, I don't dare.

'CAPTAIN OF ARTILLERY'

A girl from our cell has been before the judges. She comes back very concerned.

'I finally know what I'm accused of. Wearing a Republican overall, having a pistol, and the attack on La Montaña barracks.[11] What I regret is not having actually been there. If I knew what they were like, yours truly would have been the first to pick up a rifle...'

'If all the people detained for "having attacked the La Montaña barracks" had in fact done so, it wouldn't have lasted five minutes,' says a woman.

'What about López Ochoa's body?' another one joins in.[12] 'If everyone shot or condemned to death for having, as they say, "profaned the dead body of General López Ochoa", had really

27

done it, they'd have had to queue up longer than we do for water in Ventas...'

'That judge "El Chino" doesn't need you to be accused of anything to hand down the death sentence. Any Red who goes before him gets the death penalty.'

An old illiterate peasant woman, wearing a headscarf and full skirts, who has come to have Clara write a letter for her, decides to add her pennyworth:

'Well, I've been accused of "commandating" the artillery. I don't even know what that is. A poor old woman like me, who can't even read or write!'

'She's accused of being a captain of artillery during the war,' Clara explains.

This is so grotesque I don't know whether to be indignant or to laugh out loud. How can anybody be so cynical as to claim that this poor old woman could have been an artillery captain? Could a military judge accept such an accusation? A court made up of professional military men? Impossible.

'Don't worry, grandma. As soon as he sees you, the judge will set you free.'

'Set me free?' the old woman exclaims. 'I've been tried at Las Salesas and given twelve years and a day!'

'On one wing,' Clara tells me, 'there's a sixty-two-year-old woman. She's been on trial and sentenced to twelve years and a day, accused... of being a member of the Girls' Union.'

No comment.

A 'REMOVAL'

A sad 3 May!

The news from the world outside is bad: after making short work of the Maginot Line, Nazi troops have occupied France in only a few days. This hits us like a bombshell. But it will take more than that to destroy the hopes of the prisoners in Ventas. The conviction that Hitler and his minions will be crushed is so strong that no one panics. 'Either way, they're going to get more of a beating than a carpet ...' And with this tranquil sense of confidence, the inmates continue their normal prison life as if nothing had happened.

That's what is so extraordinary in Ventas. In here, where torture and executions are our daily bread, the women, after a 'removal' or a catastrophic piece of news, once the first few moments of despair have passed, find a way to start talking again quite calmly. Basically, if you think about it, this is quite natural. Because difficult moments are so endless that, if we don't wipe them from our minds, we'd be constantly tearing our hair out, and no nervous system could withstand it for three weeks.

Clara came back to the cell at nightfall, looking very pale and silent. Unusually for her, she listens impassively to an argument between two women over a bit of space.

'Aren't you feeling well?' I ask.

'There's nothing wrong with me,' she replies shortly, not looking at me.

We gradually spread out our mats to sleep. All of a sudden, a distraught young woman rushes into the cell:

'They're "removing" María del Rey. They're putting her in the chapel right now.'

María del Rey! I can see her broad, dark-complexioned face and prominent cheekbones, her healthy, woman of the people look. 'It's not true, it can't be true,' I tell myself despairingly. An anecdote, a mere detail, comes to my mind. A few weeks ago, they took us out into the yard. A bird came and settled near us, and then flew off over the walls. María del Rey gazed after it, and in her eyes was an expression that still hurts when I recall it. That bird was life, freedom.

'You should have kept quiet about it,' Clara reproached her gently. 'You should have spared the wing for the night.'

Her words suddenly clarify things.

'You knew.'

'Yes. But I preferred to go through the anguish alone. It's not the same knowing the following day, when everything has happened, as it is to live through a "removal" night.'

It's true. A 'removal night' is something you have to have experienced to be able to understand. Realising that a woman we know, who only a few hours ago has been talking to us, has been here alive, intact, full of energy, and who within a few hours will be a dead body full of bullet holes in the Cementerio del Este, and that there is absolutely nothing we can do to prevent it, is a torment it seems impossible for a human being to bear. And as the minutes and hours go slowly by in this agonising night, we are aware that implacably, inexorably, every hour, every minute brings the dreadful moment closer: the dogs howling, the lorry, the brief silence, gunshots, the *coups de grâce*... No, really, it would be impossible for me to describe all that.

It is still dark when the lorry pulls up at the prison. Two girls in the cell cover their ears with their hands, sobbing. Clara is standing stock still, white as a ghost. And suddenly I feel I can't take it anymore; that I'm going to shout, to weep, that I can't control my nerves anymore. Unable to contain myself, I rush out of the cell towards the toilet: I don't want to hear it! I don't want to hear it!

That evening, as always when there is a 'removal', the choir has not sung.

THE CHOIR

The choir is another wonderful creation of the imprisoned teachers, a worthy addition to the school. In it the inmates learn more about Spanish folklore, one of the richest and most varied in the world. Thanks to the choir, crude or vulgar songs have been banished from the prison.

Serious Castilian songs alternate with joyous 'pandeiradas' and melancholy 'alalás' from Galicia; the virile jotas with the rhythmic sardana.

Each inmate brings with her the tunes of her home region. There are some girls from Santander, who used to sing in the Coral Montañesa choir and have been detained for 'conspiracy'. They have enriched the choir's repertoire with songs from the mountains, each one more beautiful than the last. A girl from Barcelona has taught some Catalan songs, and I witness the strange sight of women from Vallecas and Puente Toledo very enthusiastically joining in:

> *The young men from Sant Boi*
> *Are all very handsome...*

I also really enjoy discovering a truly beautiful song from Zamora that's a real gem:

> *In Samir de los Caños*
> *You gave me water*
> *As cold as snow*
> *From the mountains...*

What a magnificent musical tradition Spain has! you think when you hear such different and fine melodies.

The time for roll call is approaching. Doña Justa, the conductor of the choir, announces as usual:

'One more and that's it. Which one do you want?'

And as on every day, Matilde Revaque's lovely deep voice replies: 'The Lope de Vega.'[13]

The teacher raises the pencil that serves as her baton and at her signal, the choir begins to sing:

> *Ever since you left,*
> *My life, sun of suns,*
> *The birds don't sing*
> *The river doesn't run.*
> *Oh! My love!...*

MARIANÍN

Marianín is a very pale boy, with huge black eyes as sad as an old man's. Even though he must be about three years old, he doesn't speak, crawls everywhere, doesn't play, doesn't laugh. Every day we see him with his mother in the yard where we go to get some sun. Every so often Clara brings him a bit of something to eat: a hunk of bread, half an apple, which Marianín devours without a word. He has gradually come to trust us and got into the habit of sitting next to us.

Somebody has told us that this boy was brutally tortured by the Falangists. Clara steers the conversation in that direction. His mother's face darkens.

31

'My poor child!' she exclaims. 'When I was arrested, in order to make me talk they put him naked face down on a table and several thugs started whipping him, until his back was red raw. The poor little mite was only two. Look,' she sees, lifting up his top to show his emaciated torso. His back is covered in long violet scars.

As she does this, the little boy gives an inarticulate cry and starts trembling, overcome by a real sense of terror. He waves his little hands frantically. His mother kisses and hugs him tenderly:

'Don't be afraid, my life, my soul, no one's going to hurt you...'

Turning to us, she explains, tears in her eyes:

'I can't talk about it in front of him. Even though he doesn't speak, he understands everything, and whenever I explain what happened in the "*checa*", he gets like this and then I have a hard job calming him...'[14]

At that precise moment, two men dressed in black cross the yard. One of them is casually carrying a small roughly made wooden casket. Complete silence falls, and some of the old women cross themselves.

'One less Red seed, "Veneno" will say,' I think bitterly.

DOÑA PEPITA

A girl from our wing arrives, looking very pale and agitated.

'They called Doña Pepita to the governor's office while she was at Mass.'

This brings a chorus of despairing cries:

'If they called her like that, it can't be good news.'

'Something must have happened to her children.'

Doña Pepita is a woman always in mourning, who still has the remains of a great beauty. Widowed at a young age with two very young boys, she never wanted to remarry – although not for want of offers – preferring to devote her life to her children. They were all she lived for, depriving herself of everything a young woman could have asked of life, working hard to bring them up. A profound believer, her only refuge was religion. Her sons were good, hard-working, intelligent, and loved their mother dearly. Thanks to great sacrifices she managed to provide them with some education. Doña Pepita gave thanks to God from the bottom of her heart. Her sacrifices were well rewarded.

The war broke out. Her sons, ardent Republicans, joined wholeheartedly on the side of the people. In 1939, all three of them were arrested by the Francoists. Doña Pepita was sentenced to twenty years. Her two sons, to death.

'My sons won't be shot. God will not allow it!' Doña Pepita always said, trusting blindly in him. To beg for this mercy, she spends all day in the chapel, endlessly praying, offering novena after novena, and taking communion every day. Now she's been called to the prison governor's office. In Ventas, we all know what that means.

'Here she comes,' one woman says in a low voice.

Doña Pepita appears in the entrance to the wing, her face shaded by her black mantilla. Mortally pale, she is walking like an automaton, gazing into the distance without a single tear.

There's a deathly silence. No one dares ask.

Eventually the 'trusty' goes up to her.

'Which one?' she asks quietly.

'Both of them. Tomorrow morning,' Doña Pepita whispers hoarsely.

A horrified murmur. It's an unbearable sight.

Somebody tries to take her by the arm. Doña Pepita shakes her off firmly. She walks bolt upright between us and enters the cell. All at once she collapses onto her sleeping mat and starts to shout with searing pain:

'There is no God! It's all a lie! There is no God, there is no God!'

That night, Clara gets up several times to go to the toilet. The last time, seeing she is taking a long while to return, I go to see what's happening. I meet her in the corridor.

'Is something wrong?'

We reach the washbasins by the toilet. There, sitting on a crate, is Doña Pepita, staring into space, arms folded across her chest as if cradling a child. She doesn't even notice we are there.

Clara nods her head in the direction of the toilet, and I realise what she is so worried about. In there is a thick rope for hanging washing on. That is what Doña Pepita is staring at...

All that night, Clara and I come and go to the toilets. We meet many other women from our wing, brought there by the same concern.

The next morning, someone has removed the rope. And yet for several long nights, Doña Pepita stays awake in the toilets and the entire wing stands guard anxiously around her.

'EVER SINCE YOU LEFT'

Yesterday they came for Matilde Revaque. She behaved courageously.

'I hope you all get a reprieve, comrades,' she told the women sentenced to death. 'But if you have to go, don't give them the satisfaction of seeing you tremble.'

'Hey, no speeches here!' she is brutally interrupted by Victoria, the head guard, who once worked under her.

Matilde studies her coldly.

'I'm going to be shot because in the Republic I held the same position as you do under Franco. That should lead you to show me more respect.'

That evening, the choir sang again. We all sang half-heartedly, without energy or joy. Matilde was highly thought of in Ventas.

Doña Justa is pale and serious.

'One more and that's it,' she says, her voice choking. 'Which one do you want?'

'The Lope de Vega,' a youthful voice responds.

Who was the first to get to their feet? Impossible to say. As if on a spring, we all leap up. Profoundly moved, we sing the song, without tears but resolutely, as if taking an oath.

From that moment on, 'Ever Since You Left' has always been sung standing up in Ventas. Lope de Vega's melancholy poem has been transformed into a battle cry, a song of unity, of homage to our female comrades who have fallen at the hands of the enemy.

A COWARD

In mid-morning, an official appears, to tell me I have a visitor. Can it be possible? I leap down the steps to the visiting room two by two. About twenty noisy, rushing inmates are crowding in the doorway, and soon after at least thirty people appear from the opposite direction. I look for my supposed visitor, and suddenly give a cry of joy: it's M.

M. and I have been friends since we were children. Our friendship is fraternal, solid, and healthy, although not exempt from bitter arguments and frequent clashes. We both have frank, almost insolent characters and a strong temperament, never hesitating when it comes to 'telling each other some home truths'. The Francoist uprising caught him in the Nationalist zone. Until today, I had no idea what his fate had been.

I find him changed, thinner, with a previously unknown harshness in his eyes and a bitter crease at the corners of his lips. When he sees me, he doesn't make any gesture or smile. Seeing me must have made a great impact on him.

What is he saying to me? I can see his lips moving, but I'm separated from him by two rows of bars, in between which 'Pasos Largos' (Long Strides) is walking, ears pricked, and the deafening noise in the room means I can't understand his words. All of a sudden, behind him and almost right up against him, I see a Falangist – an effeminate expression, a pale face crossed by the brief brushstroke of a small black moustache – who is looking at each of us in turn and seems to be listening closely to what M. is telling me. What is this Falangist doing here, when he is plainly not visiting anyone? It's obvious: he's keeping an eye on M., and has perhaps been following him. How can I tell M. that this individual is standing right behind him? In vain I wait anxiously for the Falangist to be distracted in some way so that I can gesture discreetly to M. All at once, some inmates who were right next to me move further away. There's relative silence and I can clearly hear M. speaking. He's insulting me. Not in the tone of a friendly rebuke. No: from enemy to enemy, with premeditation, precision, and cuttingly ('I would never have thought you could sink so low...').

I see red. My response is so brutal I myself am surprised at the sound of my voice.

M. turns round to the Falangist, an ironic smile on his lips, and the two exchange a knowing look.

'You see how arrogant she is?' says M.

All of a sudden, I comprehend with absolute clarity the meaning of this hateful scene. M. is demonstrating to a person of note his absolute submission to the regime of the yoke and arrows.[15] 'Let's go and see a Red I know…,' he must have told him, and his insults are nothing more than a kind of guarantee, a 'proof' of his complete adhesion to Francoism. He is a repugnant coward.

Spitting nails, I run through the wings of the prison until I'm out of breath, back to our cell. My companions gather round me, curious to know what happened.

'Who was it?'

'A swine.'

Trembling with indignation, I tell them everything in hasty phrases, stumbling over myself.

'A few days ago,' one of the girls says, 'one of the women sentenced to death was visited by her cousin, who is high up in the Falange, a "chief" as they call them. "I haven't come to commute the death sentence," he told her, "and I don't intend to do anything to save your body. But I want to save your soul; and so that you can be reconciled to God in your remaining days on earth, I've brought you a copy of *The Imitation of Christ*…".'

I could feel my cheeks burning as if I had been slapped. Not so long ago, that book by Thomas à Kempis had been one of my favourites.

I don't mention this. Later, in the night, I can't sleep, tossing and turning as I go over my conversation with M. in my mind. Suddenly I remember him as a sincere, honest and generous youngster. Francoism has turned him into 'that'…

And this degradation seems to me even more unforgivable than all the torture and executions.

CHRISTIAN CHARITY

The arrival of the Buen Pastor nuns brought with it some changes in Ventas.

The prison guards still continue with the roll call, 'removing' people in the middle of the night, and carrying out the same brutal repression of the inmates. Thanks to many transfers, the nuns have cleared all the corridors, toilets, yards and so on, and are keeping us all under lock and key in our cells. Together with the dreadful chaos of the early days, we have also lost certain advantages. It's goodbye to coming and going in the corridors, to conversations in the yards, staying on one's mat when it's time for Mass. The nuns have got us properly locked in, with no communication between the different wings. We can only go down into the yards when it's our turn, and in single file. And we are forcibly obliged to attend Mass.

The first Sunday it was celebrated by 'El Gato Montés' (the Wild Cat) – a young priest with unruly hair who it's said was hidden among the Republican ranks. At first there was silence. But suddenly 'El Gato Montés' turned brusquely to confront us.

'You women,' he shouted in a stentorian voice, 'who are here expiating your crimes...'

This led to an uproar. The prisoners started muttering, protesting out loud. An old woman next to me couldn't contain herself.

'They talk about our crimes, but what do they do? They've executed my husband and son!'

The result: with their sweet Christian charity, the nuns cut off all communication for the prison: no parcels, no visits. This lasted for over a month.

They also refused to allow the women spending their last night in the chapel the meagre consolation of being accompanied by other prisoners. Catechists, nuns, and the priest spend that terrible night harassing the condemned inmate to get her to confess, adding this fresh, refined torture to their cruel agony. They use the vilest kind of blackmail to achieve their aims.

That is what they did with Julia Lázaro.

Julia, a communist, was pregnant when she was condemned to death. The Francoists waited until she gave birth. She had a girl more beautiful than the sun. Two months later, a guard came looking for her one evening on some pretext or other. Julia who was about to breastfeed her baby, left her in the arms of a companion.

'They're going to "remove" me.'

'No, Julia, why would they come at this time of day?' the others protested.

But she was taken at once to the chapel, and the repugnant blackmailing began immediately:

'Make a confession and we'll have the child brought in so that you can feed her.'

'No.'

The baby girl's cries grew louder and louder until they reached the chapel.

'Why won't you confess?'

Julia eyed them scornfully:

'I'm a committed communist: I don't believe in God and I won't confess.'

This hateful scene continued all through the night: the anguished cries of the baby girl, the nuns insisting and insisting...

Julia did not give way. As a reprisal, in the morning the nuns took the baby to La Inclusa foundling home. When the family came to recover her, they found the girl had disappeared. What can have happened to her?

SERAFINES AND JUAN MARCH'S MAN

At the head of the nuns is the 'White Eminence', Mother Superior María de las Serafines. She is a German nun and is obviously a Gestapo agent. Her icy stare produces real physical discomfort. Serafines has no emotions; there's not the slightest human trait in her. She is the cold, implacable political enemy, organised and meticulous. She has a very famous notebook in which she writes the name of every inmate, together with a short biography. She has an astonishing memory. With her, there is no escape.

'You are So-and-So,' she says. 'You are on such and such wing, in such and such cell. So explain to me why I find you in a wing that isn't yours.'

The woman tries to justify herself. A hopeless task.

'Your wing receives visitors on such and such day. You are banned from receiving any. Next time I will take more severe measures.'

It is with her that systematic mass checks are brought in, as well as the constant shifting of inmates from one wing to another. Serafines wants to eliminate any possibly of organisation. Her obsession is the communists; she will go to any lengths to uncover them. Some repugnant characters, such as Vives, follow her orders and give her a daily bulletin. In spite of this, the jealous servant of

38

the madman of Berchtesgaden obtains very poor results. All the inmates are watchful.

As if we don't have enough with her, the Ventas fauna has been enriched with another fine specimen: Eugenio Vargas, alias 'Tío Nene', the brand-new prison governor. Eugenio Vargas is the prison guard who helped Juan March escape under the Republic.[16] Known as 'the last pirate of the Mediterranean', March has rewarded his trustworthy friend by offering him this position at Ventas, which brings with it substantial benefits. Officially, there are many items of food that come into the prison for the inmates. But they 'get lost' along the way, and instead of ending up in our empty stomachs, they arrive at the Economato, where the prisoners have to pay for them in cash at very elevated prices. So while 'Tío Nene' struts around, increasingly pot-bellied and smug, belching out hateful words, we inmates grow thinner for all to see, and the infirmary is full to overflowing.

THE NINE REPRIEVES

Unexpectedly this evening our wing has been called to the yard. When we arrive, we find all the prisoners condemned to death lined up in front of us. What's going on?

Standing in the middle of the yard are the governor, the head guard, a tall, good-looking priest, other people we don't know, and the Mother Superior with her horrible false teeth.

The handsome priest steps forward, a piece of paper in his hand, gestures elegantly and says with a smile:

'We have good news for you. I have a long list of prisoners who are to be reprieved.'

Everyone holds their breath. A hundred women condemned to death are waiting. I avoid looking them in the eye.

But what's this? Following this sensational announcement, all the dignitaries start chatting again with lots of little smiles and smug comments, without the slightest regard for the condemned women who are waiting silently, immobile and dignified.

Finally, the priest waves the sheet of paper again and reads out a name:

'Prisoner So-and-So.'

Her face deadly pale, the woman indicated steps out of the lines of those condemned to death. They gesture for her to approach, and with disdainful condescension ask her question after question in a leisurely fashion. She barely answers.

This goes on for some time, until the priest makes up his mind to read the second name on the list. The same ceremony takes place. They all smile and pass comments, as if a hundred condemned women were not standing there, waiting for the word their lives depend on.

Now they have read nine reprieves and they're still chatting and joking among themselves for several minutes that seem to us like centuries.

After a long while, and as though he were saying something completely unimportant, the priest turns to us and says casually: 'That's all,' waving his refined fingers.

One woman utters a piercing wail and collapses, with an attack of nerves. She is one of the reprieved.

TO LAS SALESAS

Yesterday they took us to Las Salesas, where we had to appear before an 'emergency' court martial.

By now we all know what to expect when it comes to Francoist 'justice'. And yet, in spite of everything, it's hard to believe that in the mid-twentieth century there can be such an incredible mockery of every human right.

Almost a hundred of us were judged together. We had one defence lawyer between us. And when I say defence lawyer I should put it in quotation marks, because it would take a leap of the imagination to believe that this gentleman was there to defend us. We had never seen him before the trial, and never, either before, after or during the hearing had we exchanged a single word with him. We never got to know his name, and the only image we keep of him is that of a desperately bored gentleman covering his mouth with his hand to discreetly stifle his constant yawns.

The interrogation of the first defendant begins: he faces a deluge of questions. But no sooner has he begun a response that demolishes the arguments of the accusation than a stentorian 'Be quiet!' cuts him short.

'Why ask me questions if you won't let me answer?' he declares.

He has hardly finished saying this when, at a gesture from the presiding judge, a pair of guards haul him off to the holding cell, from which he will only re-emerge to hear he has been condemned to death.

Another prisoner, who is completely illiterate, discovers to his stupefaction he is accused of editing a Republican newspaper.

'How can I have edited a newspaper when I don't know how to read or write?' he protests.

No matter! The court has no compunction about sentencing him to thirty years and a day. The 'defence lawyer' says nothing. (Because in quite a few of the cases, after the interrogation, the defence lawyer pipes up, between two yawns, with a sleepy 'The defence has nothing to add, your honour', as fresh as a daisy).

One man tries to say he was tortured: 'to the cells!' Another, who is gravely ill, has a blackout: 'to the cells'.

Between the two sessions, we are met with a disagreeable surprise: there's no food for us.

'If any of you have money,' the guard suggests when we protest, 'you can have food brought from the restaurant.'

But since none of us has a peseta, there's nothing for it but to go hungry.

All of a sudden, a guard appears with a package in his hand.

'So-and-So, a package from your family.'

The woman in question takes the package and shares a knowing look with us. She doesn't have a family or even know anyone in Madrid.

We share the food out evenly. There's not much, but it tastes delicious. Who will ever know your name, man or woman from Madrid, who, defying the repression, sends us this generous message of solidarity?

A huge number of death sentences were handed down that day. It's tough, but our spirits remain high.

'WE SHALL CRUSH THEM!'

There's been a long series of transfers. A lot of women previously sentenced to death, including Matilde Landa, have been sent to

Palma de Mallorca prison. Clara also left, and I had no more news of her, as correspondence between prisons is prohibited. A lot of my companions have lost their lives in front of a firing squad: Clarita de Pablo, who looked as if she came straight out of a Romero de Torres[17] painting and who had just turned twenty; Elena Cuartero, who was over fifty; the Orozco sisters and many, many more... it's a long list.

At the moment I am in one of the school basements, where most of us students are housed, as well as all the teachers. The atmosphere here is pleasant.

Two young girls, communists who have not yet been tried, have been taken out for 'inquiries'. This has caused a great stir. It's been a while since anybody was questioned. Comments fly round the room: the two girls are much appreciated, and we're concerned about their fate.

All of a sudden, the basement door opens, and a woman appears, pale, upset, overcome with emotion. She has just had a visitor. When they see how she looks, all the conversations come to an abrupt halt.

'What's wrong?'

In the complete silence her words are like a whiplash:

'Hitler has attacked the Soviet Union.'

There's a violent reaction. All of us leap to our feet. As one, in an indescribable fervour, communists, socialists, anarchists, those without a party, young and old, we rush out of the basement. In the corridors, crowds of inmates from every wing, driven by the same impulse, are running from side to side, ignoring the guards, not even hearing the screams of the 'Ametralladora' (Machine-Gun), of 'Marina y Aire' (Navy and Air Force) and Cabrera, threatening terrible punishments if we don't immediately return to our mats.

'We shall crush them!'

This is the unanimous cry from Ventas prison. A cry that emphasises the deep-rooted, moving confidence everyone in the prison has in the country of socialism, a confidence obvious even in those who not long ago were fiercely critical of the German–Soviet pact. Never before has there been such a poignant moment of frank camaraderie, of unity.

In the light of these events, the removal of the two communists for 'inquiries' is clear: it's no coincidence that 'they' have chosen precisely today to submit them to torture. The authorities were 'celebrating' the news in their own way.

The two girls came back forty-eight hours later, badly beaten, their bodies covered with bruises, but still smiling and resolute:

'They beat us in front of the judge himself,' they explain.

Vehemently supported by the entire basement, the two of them go to see the prison governor and the Mother Superior. They show them the marks of their torture, and strongly demand a protest is made through legal channels for such brutal treatment. Astonished at their audacity, the governor agrees to pass on the protest. It's the first time this has happened in Ventas.

This significant event emphasises an indisputable fact: the extraordinary historical event we are living has changed the physiognomy of the prison.

And indeed, when we say not 'The Soviet Union will crush them', but simply 'We shall crush them', we are unconsciously expressing our deepest feelings. We're not mere spectators of the conflict, but more like another unit in that great army: a unit that might be under siege, but which continues fighting against the enemy, making our contribution to the common struggle. And this feeling, which we cannot define but which beats in all our hearts, gives us a new, previously unsuspected strength.

The inmates' attitude is both resolute and serene. Nobody shows any fear. Nor do they talk about the horror of war, what it might mean for the Soviet people. Is this because we are indifferent to it, monstrously selfish? To suggest that would be an insult. How could we of all people be insensitive to the pain of others? Our feeling is more complex. It is like the combatant who in the heat of battle continues his advance through a hail of bullets, without pausing in his charge to bend over his brothers-in-arms falling all round him, to whom however he is united by the closest of links.

In all honesty, this feeling is also mixed with a little envy. They are fighting face to face, rifle in hand. We are unarmed.

'How well I understand now the German volunteers in the International Brigades,' somebody says beside me.[18]

It's true. Even for me, who has never so much as picked up a rifle, how wonderful it would be to be firing at the enemy right now! A bullet for every execution, for every tortured woman, for every 'Cara al Sol' sung, for every humiliation suffered!

The next morning, not at dawn as usual but quite a bit later, thunderous gunfire startles us all: in the nearby Cementerio del Este: Domingo Girón, Eugenio Mesón and Guillermo Ascanio, all three of them communists, have just been executed with percussion bullets. The Francoists are commemorating in their own fashion the cowardly attack by the Hitlerian hordes on the country of socialism.

THE MOTHER

'Peque' ('Titch'), Brígida Jiménez, is my friend. A woman of the people through and through, she has wonderful common sense, a fearsome temper; she is afraid of nothing and nobody, and conceals beneath her rough exterior a sensitive, generous heart. When some official or other addresses her, Peque raises the short body she has been endowed with, furrows her terrible brow, and fixes her with a look of inimitable insolence. I can just see her in her Republican overalls, grasping her rifle. But I have to imagine it, because Peque is the person least inclined to boast or confide that I know.

Somebody told me an anecdote that presents a complete portrait of her. This was back in the dark two years of the Second Republic.[19] As a young woman, Peque was out on the street selling the clandestine *Mundo Obrero* (Workers' World) newspaper. Suddenly, two policemen appeared and arrested her.

'Hey, kid, come with us to the station. Hand over the newspapers.'
Peque didn't bat an eyelid.
'Okay, let's go to the station. But I'll carry the newspapers.'

They had been walking a good while when suddenly they came across a group of workmen leaving a job. Quick as a flash, Peque flung the newspapers at them.

'It's *Mundo Obrero*! Catch it! Take it!'

When the two cops reached the police station with her, Peque cheekily denied the facts:

'It's a lie! Tell me, where are the newspapers they say I had? Show me them.'

Whenever our wing has visitors, Peque is top of the list. It's her mother who comes to see her. She sends her small packages, packages of the poor, with a blackish ration loaf, and a tiny tortilla, or a bit of sardine, that miserable little fish the poor people of Madrid now eat. When the package includes an orange or apple, Peque rejoices:

'My, oh my! My old ma is in the money!'

Despite her reluctance to speak, whenever she talks of her mother, one can tell how profoundly she must love her. 'My old ma is worth her weight in gold,' she often says. Coming from her, that's equivalent to the most enthusiastic demonstration of a child's love.

She never eats the contents of these tiny packages on her own. I'm often the beneficiary of her generosity. 'Here,' she says, breaking a sad little roll in two. And at the slightest hesitation: 'Don't be shy. Eat it up.'

Today, we have visitors. The employee arrives with the first list. And without fail, Peque is on it. And among the last of them, a surprise: my name is there. Taken aback, I go up to the official:

'There must be some mistake, I didn't...'

But Peque pushes me forward cheerily.

'Get in there. It's my old ma. I told her to put you down.'

Disconcerted, confused, not knowing exactly what's going on, I enter the visiting room, where there's an indescribable racket going on. Peque drags me to one end of the room. Two sets of bars away stands a tall, thin woman with kind, light-coloured eyes, wrapped in a threadbare black shawl that covers her head and shoulders: Peque's mother.

While Peque is explaining something with gestures and expressive signs, I stand beside her, silent, immobile, unable to control my emotion. Whenever her mother looks at me or says something, I don't understand, all I can do is smile.

The guard goes to the far end where some women are screaming wildly. Quick as a flash, Peque takes advantage to ask: 'How is the Russian front going?' A sly smile lights up her mother's weary face, suddenly making it look strangely youthful. With her hand she makes the gesture of thrashing someone. 'We're giving them hell,' she says, then her face quickly becomes impassive once more: the guard is back.

When eventually, despite our vehement protests ('But we've only just come in!') we are all turfed out of the visiting room, the two of us leave for our wing arm-in-arm. Peque is grumbling indignantly: 'That scum won't even let you talk, kept behind bars as if we were wild animals in the Retiro zoo...'

'Peque has nothing of her own,' the other women often say. It's true. She shares everything. Even her mother's affection. And I suddenly think that never, since I was born, have I received such a convincing proof of friendship as the one this young girl from Madrid has shown me.

I'd like to tell her so. But all my thoughts are translated into a clumsy 'Thank you, Peque'. A no-nonsense 'Be quiet, silly', puts an end to my effusiveness.

'Your mother,' I say to her later, 'reminds me of a character in a novel I read during the civil war: *The Mother* by Gorky.'

Peque smiles, and there's a glint of pleasure in her eyes:

'My sister had that book. It's a good book.'

A SINK IS BLOCKED

A sink is blocked in the school basement. Unfortunately for us, tomorrow it's our turn to receive visitors, and it's 'Veneno' who is carrying out the inspection. Nothing escapes her tiny, evil creature's eyes, and she soon spots the problem.

She stands there triumphantly, hands on hips.

'Listen, you Red riffraff,' she says, raising her forefinger. 'If this sink isn't cleared by tomorrow morning, the wing won't have any visitors.'

As the hours go by and all our efforts are in vain, the women become increasingly dismayed. By now it's almost nightfall, and we are still struggling with bits of wire and anything else we can find to unblock the sink, but without success.

'The only thing to do is to get a nail and a stone and make a hole in the wastepipe to get rid of the blockage,' one woman says firmly.

We all look at her: it sounds like a good idea.

'If "Veneno" turns up and sees us making a hole, she'll ban us from having visitors for six months.'

'That's true. So what can we do?'

'We'll have to do it at night,' another woman suggests.

A girl with curly hair has an idea:

'I think there's a solution. You all go to bed as usual. I'll stay in the toilet and smash the pipe. If I'm caught, none of you knew anything about it, and I'll be the only one to lose visiting rights. I have no family anyway, so the punishment will be meaningless.'

It's not bad: we all look at each other.

'I agree,' says a youthful voice. 'But on one condition: I'm staying with you.'

'But why? You do have family that comes to visit you.'

'Well, because I feel like staying with you.'

We're all touched by this. The curly-haired girl is a communist; the other one, an anarchist. So the offer acquires a deeper meaning.

That night we all go to bed. On the two girls' mats, we put two dummies made from our cloth bags and blankets, carefully tucked up. We hear repeated muffled blows from the toilets. One inmate keeps her eye on the lock to the basement to avoid any surprise. Everybody holds their breath. Minutes that seem like centuries drag by.

All at once the two girls burst cheerfully into the basement.

'We've done it!'

Seeing them like this, hugging one another and smiling, we all rejoice. Suffering from the harshest repression, the unity that the enemy managed to break for a moment, is now being patiently restored.

Thirty seconds later, the basement door opens. Serafines herself is doing the rounds.

Under our blankets, we all stifle a tremendous desire to laugh.

PEQUE IS TAKEN FOR 'INQUIRIES'

Peque is taken out for 'inquiries'. It's a brutal, unexpected piece of news. We all surround her, helping her to roll up her mat, to put her few belongings in bags. Of all of us, she is the one who receives the news most calmly, without any useless fuss.

The guard is already outside in the corridor, hurrying her up. The inmates all hug her.

'Good luck, my girl. Get out soon.'

I am the last to approach her. Peque lifts her hands and lays them on my shoulders. At that moment, a wave of emotion shows in her light blue eyes that makes her look incredibly like her mother.

'Tell ma to keep her spirits up,' she says in a voice I don't recognise.

She strides off down the corridor, head held high. I'm losing my little prison sister. I'm also losing the mother. I'll no longer see her tall figure in mourning, her kindly smile, in the visiting room.

I feel literally stunned.

THE LITTLE SNEAK THIEF

The room for 'consumptives' or infirmary is where the most distressing cases in the prison are to be found. Here you see all the recognised tuberculosis sufferers, as well as some cases of cancer and other incurable diseases. Inmates usually leave the infirmary in a wooden box.

Despite this and the sick women's physical exhaustion, they remain in good spirits and there are moments when they find a way to have fun.

One of the liveliest among them is Conchi, a young sneak thief who has tuberculosis.

'Tell me,' she asks, 'if you had to steal this box,' – she shows a medium-sized one – 'where would you hide it?'

'We're political prisoners. We're not interested in learning how to steal,' replies an irritated voice.

'Leave us in peace with your tricks.'

But that's not enough to put Conchi off. She hides a little behind her bed, then appears in front of us, doing pirouettes:

'I've got it on me!' she cries triumphantly, waving her pleated skirt. 'Where is it?'

And with that she twirls round as if she is doing a waltz, and jumps up and down the steps leading to the terrace, laughing out loud at our astonishment.

Eventually she takes the box out from under her skirt – she was clutching it between her legs – and hands it to an inmate.

'Take it.'

The other woman refuses it angrily. This doesn't offend Conchi, who laughs even more.

A woman from the basement pays me a visit and brings us wonderful news: the Red army has gone on the attack and launched an irresistible offensive. The Germans are retreating as fast as they can.

All the women crowd round her, hugging one another, laughing and crying at the same time.

'I told you so.'

'Now we really will crush them.'

'They're capable of taking revenge on our men, that scum,' says one old woman.

'That's true. "Those people" are capable of anything.'

Yes, we all know only too well how the Francoists 'celebrate' the ups and downs of the war. The circle of women splits up.

I pick up a blanket and go out for a while onto the empty terrace. Conchi follows and sits with me on the blanket. She is silent and looks worried.

'Do you think?' she says finally, her voice scarcely more than a whisper, 'that they'll do something to the men?'

'It could well be.'

Conchi shivers.

'I'm really scared for my husband. He's in Porlier.'

I burst out laughing.

'No, silly. We were talking about the political prisoners, not the others.'

'My husband isn't a thief!' she protests angrily. Her eyes fill with tears. 'He's political... he was a commissar during the civil war.'

I'm so surprised I'm left speechless for a moment.

'Really? And you...?'

'Yes, I am a thief,' she mutters bitterly.

'I never used to steal, you know,' she goes on after a lengthy silence. 'I used to do honest work. My husband was from my neighbourhood and we loved each other blindly. We were married in 1938. Then Casado's people put him in jail – they served him up on a plate to Franco.[20] I had just given birth. Because I had no money, they threw me out of our flat, after I had sold or pawned everything there was. With my daughter in my arms, I went round sleeping in doorways, in Metro entrances, washing where I could, begging for money when I got too hungry... Then I fell ill. As if that wasn't enough, my husband was sentenced to death. I went to see the lawyer.'

'It's not a very complicated business,' he snapped. 'Ten thousand pesetas should see to it...'

'Ten thousand pesetas, for pity's sake! What could I do? I wandered round Madrid carrying my little one, desperate, out of my mind. I had no idea what to do: steal, sleep with the first man I came across, or throw myself and my child under a tram...'

Her voice gives out. A terrible fit of coughing shakes her wretched little body.

'So you stole?'

'Yes. And it went well. So then I carried on doing it. My baby had to be looked after, I had to take my husband his parcels...'

'Conchi, why don't you give up that life?'

Conchi looks at me with pain in her eyes and shakes her head from right to left.

'It's too late now.'

'Perhaps if...'

'No.'

'Does he know...?'

Oh, no! I tell him I'm working and earning well. The day he finds out he'll spit in my face, or throw me out, or even kill me, I don't know!' She shrugs her shoulders. 'When it comes down to it, I saved him and I saved the little one. Besides, with the little time I have left...'

THE 'THEFT' OF A PENCIL

The doctor has discharged me from the infirmary without so much as examining me.

'This one can go back to her wing.'

So, 'cured' in such an expeditious manner, I've returned to my basement.

I find all the women there in a state of great agitation. There has been a serious incident in the school, and one girl has been put into solitary.

Some explanation is necessary to describe what has happened. Some time ago the prison authorities – Mother Superior Serafines must have something to do with it – decided to provide a room (quite a decent one, it has to be said) to use as our school. In it there are benches and even a brand-new blackboard.

Such kindness on their part seemed odd to us. And so it came as no surprise when we saw installed on a sort of raised platform an official we had not seen before. This lady announced very calmly that the prison administration had decided to 'enrich' the school with a compulsory daily religious lesson, which she would be taking. From now on – she told us – to gain release on parole, we would have to prove we knew not only how to read and write but also to pass a religious exam. If we did not pass it, any application for parole would be categorically refused.

Throughout all the classes, 'Señorita María', for that's her name, stays in the school, now keeping watch from her dais, poking her nose into the lessons to see what's being taught. And at the end, she launches into a mystical sermon, concealing the many weaknesses in her explanations with the catchphrase: 'That cannot be explained, it's an article of faith', that leaves us all in stitches.

As a supreme act of charity, the prison lends pencils to those inmates in the school who don't have any. Señorita María herself distributes them at the start of classes and collects them up at the end.

This evening, when she collected them, Señorita María shouted to high heaven that, according to her, one was missing.

Our mystical religious teacher was not content with insulting the prisoners, accusing them of being thieves, but went on to grab the pencils belonging to all the other students – about sixty of them – on the pretext that they're identical to the ones she loans us: which is perfectly natural, since the only place that inmates can get pencils is by buying them at the prison Economato.

A girl with light-blue eyes, sentenced for conspiracy, rounded on her:

'You allow yourself to call us all thieves because, according to your count, there is one pencil missing. And because one is missing, you take sixty. What should we call you?'

She was immediately stripped of visiting rights, despite vehement protests from all the other inmates.

Two women from the school basement, one anarchist and the other communist, have gone to see the nuns, on behalf of all of us, to convey our request that this unjust punishment of our companion be lifted.

'Well, if she apologises to Señorita María, the punishment will be lifted,' the nuns suggest, visibly perturbed by our attitude.

'Señorita María has unjustly insulted us all, and has not apologised,' our envoys replied.

The prison authorities would not give way on their ultimatum. It's a question of principle. Serafines herself came to speak to the girl being punished. 'Why do you persist in refusing to apologise? Offer this sacrifice to God.'

'No.'

Eventually, faced with the girl's steadfast refusal, the prison authorities were the ones forced to back down. When the girl came back to the basement, her reception was ecstatic. The atmosphere is one of triumph. The besieged unit can also win battles.

Shortly afterwards, we are informed of a measure that does not come as a surprise: the basement school has been abolished. We will all be split up in different cells.

Serafines has understood the danger that a united group like ours represents.

THE PROLETARIAN ROSE

I was wrong in thinking that Peque's mother would not be back. More gaunt than ever, with a new sadness in her eyes, she comes regularly to see me when we're allowed visitors. We don't talk much: about Peque, and the war... then we fall silent. And to me, this silence between us is more wonderful than any words. Later, on my sleeping mat, I recall at length, savouring them with delight, each one of her gestures, her slightly sad smile, the little fluttering of her hand when we say goodbye...

Today is a great day. The first of May! We all dream of a procession, with banners... Some girls have received a small extra package from their homes. They're like a message sent from those outside the prison; a way of telling us that, in spite of fascism, they are not forgetting this workers' day.

Peque's mother has sent me a tiny package: a chunk of bread with the inevitable tortilla and a small round box, which I think must be a piece of fish. When I lift the lid, surprise and emotion leave me speechless. Inside, there's a rose. A velvety red rose, still fresh.

The inmates crowd round me. All their faces show intense emotion.

One of them silently ties a piece of red ribbon round the rose.

'It's our workers' rose!' a young girl shouts triumphantly.

THE POISONING ON SANTIAGO'S FEAST DAY

With great fanfare came the announcement that we were to receive an 'extraordinary ration' to celebrate the feast day of Santiago, our mutilated Spain's patron saint.

This created a great sense of expectation, as well as ironic comments.

Eventually, this stupendous 'extraordinary ration' made its solemn appearance on the wing: a slice of cod in tomato sauce.

As it has fallen apart and is not exactly abundant, the cook fishes out shreds of cod and serves them on aluminium plates.

By the time it reaches the last of us in the wing, there is nothing left but a small spoonful of bones, which we refuse.

Shortly afterwards, one woman starts crying out in pain and writhes about on the floor. Five minutes later, cries and pitiful moans are coming from all the cells. A girl from my cell goes out to see what's happening. In the middle of the corridor she suddenly hesitates, then crashes to the ground unconscious. Many more inmates are vomiting in the cells, the corridors, anywhere they can, unable to control themselves. The few of us who are unaffected raise the roof calling for help.

Shouts arise from all the wings. A few nurses go from cell to cell with an urn of herbal tea, which is apparently the only medicine the infirmary has. No doctor makes an appearance.

The nuns and guards appear not in the least bit concerned at the state of the inmates but devote all their efforts to trying to impose silence.

'Don't yell like that,' they order us. 'Your shouts can be heard out in the street...'

Good. So if they can hear us out in the street, those of us still on our feet will shout even louder.

The outcome of this hellish night has been tragic: many women have had to be taken to the infirmary in a critical condition. Others, unable to stand, have been left lying in the cells for lack of space in the infirmary.

A crime? An accident? It's hard to tell. We inmates, who know that 'they' are capable of anything, opt for an attempt at a mass poisoning. The authorities' attitude, trying to pretend nothing has happened, appears to confirm this. On this occasion, the attempt backfired on them, because outside the prison the terrible outcry of the inmates throughout the night has caused a great stir, and the entire neighbourhood is in an uproar.

The news has even reached Porlier prison, where several prisoners who are doctors have offered to come and attend us. Their offer was brutally rejected.

'The women inmates at Ventas are being perfectly well looked after,' came the cynical reply.

THE WORKSHOP

I'm in the workshop, where the Mother Superior Serafines has sent me for 'manu militari'. In this way, I 'redeem' my sentence, that's to say, I have to work eight hours a day for the much-vaunted Trust for the Redemption of Sentences through Work (Patronato de Redención de Penas por el Trabajo) for the princely sum of one peseta thirty-five cents a day. This is when we work for people outside, that is, for a series of aristocratic characters, to judge from the crowns for barons, marquises or counts sewn all over the clothes. But when we work for the aforementioned Trust for the

Redemption etc. etc., the one peseta thirty-five cents is withheld, because apparently the clothes we make are destined for prisoners and their families. Since it so happens that not a single inmate of Ventas has ever received a scrap of this clothing, and neither have our families been handed any, there are good grounds for thinking this is simply a swindle. Yet another one.

In order to achieve a good output, as well as the religious instruction with which they 'brighten' our work, the nuns don't hesitate to resort to blackmail: 'If you work hard in the workshop, you won't be transferred.'

The 'trusty' in the workshop wing is called Atanasia Alguacil. She is from Torrejón de Ardoz and has been condemned to death. Atanasia is a silent, kindly sort, always willing to help us as much as she can. Whenever our rations are bad – or more correctly, even worse than usual – Atanasia sighs sadly as she distributes them:

'Ah, my little lambs, I'm so sorry to have to serve you this garbage.'

In the workshop, there are a handful of girls who every night go to give her a kiss, as if she was their mother. Later, she goes from cell to cell tucking them up in a maternal way. One of her sons, a communist, was executed a short while ago. Her eldest is in exile.

THE NAIL

There's a girl in Ventas who has come from a provincial prison and was strictly prohibited from all contact with visitors from outside and from other inmates, during no less than five and a half months.

'How did you manage not to go mad?' I ask her.

She smiles at me.

'Don't think I wasn't close to it. It was what I was always most afraid of. In order not to completely lose my wits I took lessons every day: maths one day, geography the next, and the following one, history.'

'So you had books then?'

'Books! If only! Not a scrap of paper or pencil, not even a sewing needle. Nothing. Absolutely nothing. Apart from...'

'Apart from what?'

'I had a nail.'

'A nail?'

55

'Yes, you'll see. It was at one particularly difficult moment. They never gave me any change of clothes. They never let me go to the toilet. A rusty, foul-smelling bucket served that purpose. They only emptied it every three or four days, so you can imagine the cell didn't exactly smell of Heno de Pravia soap...'

'The guard,' she went on, 'used to give me a small jug with a litre of water 'for drinking and washing' as she made clear to me. My clothes were in an indescribable state. Since I didn't have a comb either, I would run my fingers through my hair – that was the only hairstyle I had. I didn't have a toothbrush. My fingernails grew wildly, and, given the refusal of my gaoler to let me have a pair of scissors, there was nothing left for me but to chew them conscientiously. One day I wanted to wash my knickers only in water, of course, but – something that hadn't crossed my mind – since I had nowhere to hang them, I had to go round all day with them in my hand, waving them about uselessly to try to dry them. As if that wasn't enough, I had my period. I tried asking the official for some sanitary pads, but she merely shrieked, 'stop pestering me, will you?' followed by the typical slamming of the door. I was cold. I was hungry. I was disgusted by my own body. I felt filthy, repugnant, humiliated. 'Let them shoot me once and for all,' I said to myself despairingly. I don't know what barbarity I might have committed that day. Then all at once I saw the nail. It was carefully concealed in a crack in the wall, with only its head peeping out a little. How often must I have thrown away an old nail without the slightest regret! And yet that nail – bent, rusty, without a point – made me deliriously happy. It was as if I wasn't alone in the cell, if you see what I mean. That nail saved my life. I spent almost eight days rubbing it against the cement until I'd got it straight, gleaming and with a sharp point...

'What did you do with it?'

'I made a calendar on the wall, where every day I marked the date and day of the week. I put my name above it. 'If I disappear,' I said to myself, 'someone will know I've been through here.' And that thought consoled me a little. I also used my nail to do sums to entertain myself and scratched geometrical shapes on the wall... and one day I even... No, you'll only laugh.'

'Go on, tell me.'

'One day I drew a boy's head. I don't know how to draw, and anyone seeing it would have been no more than scratches on the wall. But to me, it was my boy, the boy I would have liked to have had. I saw him, talked to him, and even gave him a name: José Luis.'

'That's a lovely name.'

The girl smiled, embarrassed.

'You asked me before if I hadn't gone crazy. As you can see, I haven't gone raving mad, but well, I'm a bit nutty,' she says mischievously.

'FAREWELL, LITTLE LAMBS!'

For the past few months, the prisoners facing the death penalty have been kept in a tiny basement, without light or ventilation. They have not been allowed to leave it, and so have been unable to see the rest of us. In the basement itself, a small altar was set up, so that they would spend what was left of their lives meditating on the afterlife and 'becoming reconciled with God', as Mother Consuelo, alias 'El bicho que picó al tren' ('The insect that stung the train') tells them.

We have no idea what fresh winds are blowing in the heights, but the fact is that in the space of a few weeks the entire basement of women condemned to death has been emptied. Executions have followed one another at a terrible rate. A few others have been reprieved.

Atanasia – who spent several weeks in the fateful basement – has returned to the wing, apparently with her sentence commuted. At least that's what the nuns have told her, but none of us believes it. Still less when we have seen that Dolores Cuevas has also been brought to our wing. She has recently been sentenced to death and has been put in the same cell as Atanasia.

'That's impossible,' our new 'trusty' Carmen told them. 'That cell is completely full.'

'Then let them squeeze together more tightly.'

Emotions are running high on the wing. We already have lengthy experience of what a demand like that means.

At nightfall I was going to fetch water from the toilets when Atanasia came up, carrying a bucket. Without thinking, and forgetting that officially she has been reprieved, I let her go first, which is what we do with condemned prisoners. She fixes her kindly, intelligent eyes on me.

'You don't believe it either, do you?' she says sorrowfully.

Confused, I mumble a vague excuse.

That night I wake up. All my cell companions are awake as well, sitting on their mattresses.

'What's going on?'

'Atanasia and Dolores Cuevas have been called "to the judges". The prison governor is here.'

Atanasia's voice can be heard from her cell.

'Why do you want me to think the judge wants to see me? I know you're taking me to the firing squad. It wasn't enough for you to execute my son. The Torrejón fascists are going to be celebrating tonight!'

The governor stammers a few words we don't understand.

Through the spyhole I manage to get a glimpse of the entrance to our wing. On one side, lurking in the semi-darkness, I can make out the paunchy, sinister figure of Juan March's accomplice, pistol in hand. Next to him, several guards form a compact, threatening group. I feel a shiver run down my spine and a dreadful feeling, a mixture of fear, anger, and, against all logic, a ridiculous sense of hope. What if a reprieve is arriving at the very last minute?

'Farewell, little lambs,' comes Atanasia's clear voice. Dolores Cuevas says nothing.

As if with one mind, all the cell doors are flung open, and the women come out into the corridor.

'Adios, Atanasia! Adios, Dolores!'

Somebody – one of 'them' – hurriedly locks the wing gate. Then the inmates give free rein to their grief. Everyone shouts; several women are close to nervous breakdowns.

A woman in my cell suddenly gets to her feet, staring wildly and making strange gestures. We all rush to restrain her. Her husband has been executed recently.

'It's Tío Nene,' says an alarmed voice.

So it is. He's accompanied by 'Morros' and 'Boris Karlof', the female guards who took the two women out.

'Silence!' roars Juan March's man. And with bestial hatred he spits filthy insults at us.

'These are the lucky ones, the ones in the workshop, with six- and twelve-year sentences! They should all be shot! Silence, I said!' Tío Nene yells, beside himself. 'Silence, or I'll bring the firing squad in!'

'Morros' backs him up.

'Let's see, where's the one who had a nervous fit? What nonsense! It's not that serious!'

'You lousy bitch!' the widow in my cell mutters in despair, trying to unburden herself. But we all keep tight hold of her before she gets into trouble.

Tonight, one woman in the wing has lost her mind. None of us knew it, but she was condemned to death and hid it so that she wouldn't have to go to the terrible basement. When she saw 'them' entering in the middle of the night, she no doubt thought they were coming for her.

THE WORKSHOP STRIKE

A few weeks ago, the nun supervising the workshop gave a few sharp taps on her desk, calling for silence:

'There is urgent work to be done. Therefore, you will have to do extra hours after supper. In return, you will receive a full plate of extra rations.'

On the first night, they did indeed bring us an abundant and tasty meal from the kitchen. The next night, it was poor and meagre. Shortly after that, it was no more than a simple cup of coffee. A few days later, even that disappeared.

The atmosphere in our wing was red hot:

'Are we going to put up with such a mockery? We have to do something.'

That night, as if on a signal, all the sewing machines suddenly came to a halt. The women sewing linen put down their needles. Those doing embroidery laid their frames on the floor.

Taken aback by this sudden silence, the nun grows restless at her desk:

'What's this? Why have you stopped?'

We all reply with one voice:

'We want the extra ration we were promised.'

Taken aback, the nun begins to wave her hands about and almost begs:

'We're having problems... We'll see what can be done...'

The women's resolute attitude bore fruit; a fairly decent, plentiful meal was hastily prepared and served to us.

That night there's a combative atmosphere on the wing.

'It's a shame Atanasia wasn't able to see this,' some of the women say sorrowfully. 'She would have been so pleased.'

FREEDOM

The Mother Superior smiles at me with her protruding false teeth that look like the keys of a sad, rented piano.

'I called you here to inform you that you are to be released.'

This comes as such a shock that I stay silent, not really comprehending what she means.

'Did you understand me?' she says in a sickly sweet voice.

She is obviously expecting a reaction: joy, gratitude, tears... I won't give her that satisfaction.

'In that case,' I say coldly, 'allow me to go and get my things and say goodbye to my companions.'

Serafines stares at me, somewhat disconcerted.

'So the news of your freedom leaves you indifferent?'

'My freedom is something normal. What isn't normal is having been kept in prison for years.'

The day before yesterday, I recall, choking back my rage, Rosita Ventura, sentenced to death, was called to this same office late in the afternoon. Not to announce her release, but to inform her she was to be executed. Rosita was a brave, beautiful woman. In Ventas, she had a two-year-old daughter, as pink and plump as a cherub. We heard the little one crying all night: Rosita refused to say confession. And at first light... The memory of this still scalds me and makes me clench my fists.

We stare at one another without a word, face to face. It's the Mother Superior who lowers her eyes first, looking down at her podgy fingers.

'God go with you,' she says curtly, without looking up.

Back on the wing, everyone rejoices. All the prisoners run to hug me, and lots give me their family's address.

'Go to my house. They don't have much money, but they won't leave you out in the street. Where three eat, so can four.'

A young woman approaches me shyly. Her husband was executed in 1939.

'If you have time,' she begs me, 'go and see my little girl. She's only four, she's very young to understand, but tell her about me, tell her I love her a lot, give her a kiss; well, you know what I mean...'

Her emotion prevents her continuing.

'Explain everything you've seen here,' another woman says. 'People outside need to know.'

'Yes.'

'Don't forget us.'

'Never!'

At the prison gate, there's a crowd of my companions from all the wings who, slipping past the guards, have come to say goodbye. Our farewells are brief and emotional. The official forces them back from the gate while she rifles through my bag.

All at once a powerful chorus rings out from the group of women crowded round the stairs:

> *Ever since you left,*
> *My life, sun of suns,*
> *The birds don't sing*
> *The river doesn't run.*
> *Oh! My love...!*

A violent emotion catches at my throat. Yes, beloved sisters, I understand the message of struggle and hope you are sending with this song of ours, the one we sing standing up in Ventas: 'Never give up the struggle, whatever happens, whatever the cost. Be worthy of all those women you have seen fall before the enemy...'

Gravely, without a word, I nod my head in what is a solemn oath. The prison official draws back the bolt. Freedom.

Free in a city I don't know, with no family and without a penny in my pocket. My only possession is a big bag, made from countless small squares of all different kinds of fabric. It took me many hours of patient work, and I'm tremendously proud of it. It even has handles!

Should I turn right? Left? There's no one in sight for me to ask. For a while, I can't decide. Then I slowly start walking to the right, at random.

All of a sudden, I see a poorly dressed young woman coming towards me with quick, small steps. She is carrying a straw basket, out of which poke some anaemic-looking leeks.

'Could you please tell me where the... neighbourhood is...?'

'Go to the Plaza de Toros and ask there,' she replies, without stopping.

I start to trot after her. She comes to a halt.

'Where is the Plaza de Toros?'

The woman looks at me in surprise.

'Don't you know Madrid?'

'No, señora.'

Her sharp eyes, very black and shining, examine me rapidly. Her gaze comes to rest on my bag.

'You've come from there, haven't you my dear?' she says, pointing her chin at the prison.

Her unexpected friendly words give me a pleasurable jolt.

'Yes.'

'How long?'

'Two years here. But I've been in other prisons.'

'Swines!'

The word resounds like a whiplash in the deserted street.

We stand looking at one another, and all at once it seems to me we've known each other a long time.

'That address you have,' she asks, 'is it your family?'

'No. I don't have family in Madrid.'

She turns towards me, her mind made up.

'Come on, I'll take you.'

'But you... you were in a hurry.'

'That's no matter! For something like this... Give me your bag.'

'What?'

'Give me your bag, I'll carry it for you.'

'But I can manage it,' I protest.

'What do you mean, woman, what do you mean? You're all skin and bone. I know they starve you to death, those sons of...'

She snatches the bag from me.

We set off walking down the silent street. On the sly, I start to study my companion. To judge from her appearance, people out of prison aren't exactly well-fed either. She is young, skinny, nervous and determined; her extremely clean clothes are badly worn. A Madrileña through and through, spirited, with a heart of gold...

I tell myself that only a very few years earlier, if someone had told me I would be talking in such a friendly and familiar way with a complete stranger in the middle of the street, it would have seemed incredible to me. 'How common!' my mother would have said. Well, why my mother? I would have said so as well. Now it turns out I am common; and in addition, I'm not in the least bit ashamed of it.

The stranger squeezes my arm.

'Why are you laughing?'

'I was remembering a stuck-up girl I used to know.'

PART II

Destined for the Crematorium

It is the 1930s, I'm in my twenties and have just finished reading a short, horrifying book: it's called *The Nazi Murder Camp of Dachau* and was written by Hans Beimler, the legendary Hans Beimler of the International Brigades, who fell in the trenches of Madrid in 1936.[1]

I read it avidly in one sitting, but with a sceptical shrug. Beimler lays it on a bit thick. The Nazis are bad people, I don't doubt that, but still…

A few years later, I will see everything in those 'murder camps' with my own eyes, and not as an onlooker but as a prisoner. Hans Beimler had fallen a long way short.

And now, will you believe me? Maybe not. But it's true and the truth must be written, although many, just like myself in the 1930s, will shrug their shoulders sceptically. I write because it must be told, even though I don't know much, with my vocabulary impoverished by exile; because it isn't about creating a literary work, it's about telling the truth. And that I can do. It riles me when people portray themselves in their memoirs as perfect heroes, who were never afraid, never thought of filling their bellies, the pure spirits! They of course were in the lead when a plan went well; but if ever there was a problem, oh no, they had already warned of it… Not me. I've been frightened, very frightened, and I have done many foolish things; I have been hungry and have even thought of stealing food from a fellow prisoner. I'll tell you everything, and I won't skirt around the truth.

CARCASSONNE AND THE FIFTH GUERRILLA GROUP[2]

Let's begin.

To find yourself a prisoner, captured by the enemy at the very last minute, when freedom seems just around the corner, is enough to make you want to tear your hair out.

Enraged, I pace back and forth in the cell – two and a half steps – like a caged lion. It's the end of May 1944, in the occupied city of Carcassonne, in the south of France. Three months later, amid the great celebrations that follow the liberation, the French will burn the hated swastika flag in public squares across the nation.

The cell walls speak a thousand words. My predecessors have filled them with inscriptions: '*On les aura*' (We will beat them!), '*Long live Communism!*', '*Long live De Gaulle!*'; the cross of Lorraine, and the hammer and sickle everywhere; emotional personal messages, written perhaps by prisoners before going to their death: 'Tell my son that...'.

Furious, I too scrawl my name, the real one, as well as something along the lines of 'Your time is nearly up, you criminals.'

True as that may be, I'm in danger of not surviving for the little time, the very short time, that they have left. For when you're caught in the Gestapo's claws, with a file labelled *terrorist Rotspanische* – Spanish Red – among others, well you can imagine.[3]

And it's lucky I wasn't caught two weeks earlier.

On 10 May, as I'm leaving work, the unforgettable Josep Ballester Soler, the *Juliol* journalist from Barcelona is waiting for me at the door. We're to go to Bram together, to interview a group of young Spaniards and hand over some propaganda.[4] Well, as I always did when I went away, that morning I left my house key with Rafaela, Rafaela Soro, a salt-of-the-earth, headstrong and plain-talking woman, afraid of nothing. My house is used by Guerrilla Command and serves as a safehouse when necessary.

Ballester is waiting for me near the station.

'You can't come, miss. There's no return train for you to get back. And you know what happened...'

Indeed, I did know, and my only pair of shoes bore the evidence. The previous week, the unexpected lack of a train home meant I had been obliged to undertake a small marathon of some 20 kilometres on foot, at great speed. At work, after a sleepless night and with the weight of 20 kilometres in my legs, I had to put up with the cheeky jibes of the cooks who assumed my sleepy state was the result of a night of debauchery.

Bram is too far away to repeat such a feat. Ballester decides to go alone; and feeling somewhat put out by the setback I go to Rafaela's house to pick up my key. When I get there, my blood runs cold: Rafaela's ramshackle old house, a guerrilla hideout, is all locked up, dead, silent. What's going on, and what can I do?

Cautiously, I get out of there, observing the surrounding area. Nothing unusual in the street. Moving swiftly, I make my way to González's, a Catalan fellow who lives nearby.

'Haven't you heard? The Germans have found the maquis in Roullens and the *noisy* ones (guerrillas) fought back with machineguns.'[5]

I freeze. González doesn't know where Rafaela is, and Rafaela has my key. And without a key, the guerrillas have no refuge. And if they're found on the street, they'll be picked up. And if... my mind is racing.

Suddenly, someone gives me a friendly slap on the back. It's José, a comrade who supplies us with identity documents that, suitably doctored, our people can use.

'Are you looking for your key?'

I grab his arm fervently.

'Do you know where it is? I need it right now.'

José listens calmly.

'We'll find you somewhere to sleep tonight. Don't worry.'

He doesn't know my house or what it is used for. I can't tell anyone. But in such a serious situation I have no choice.

'The guerrillas have to hide in my house. They've got to be able to get in.'

José considers this for less than 30 seconds and immediately sends a young lad on a bicycle to where Rafaela is. In the meantime, he and I go to a café, situated very strategically in a spot where anyone going to my house has to pass by.

Before we even get to our lookout, we both turn white. Luis (Miguel Ángel) and Antonio (known as 'El Maño'), two guerrilla leaders, emerge from my street. On their way back from the house already. A few minutes later and we wouldn't have seen them. Just thinking about it makes my heart race.

Acting naturally, José stops them and explains the situation.

They don't flinch or say a word. I'm amazed at how serenely they take the news. These two men, wanted – dead or alive – by the Gestapo, come into the café and take a seat.

A good while goes by, with them inside in a quiet corner and us outside, keeping watch; when at last the cyclist appears with the key and the four of us slowly make our way to the house. Once inside, we all heave a sigh of relief. Luis and 'El Maño' have just returned from a trip and don't know a thing. José gives them a brief rundown of events.

The gendarmes and *Wehrmacht* forces have attacked the maquis in Roullens, concealed behind the legal front of a group of *bûcherons*, charcoal burners who made charcoal from wood when they weren't touting machine guns.[6] On top of that, the Nazis have discovered a house containing photographs of the 'terrorists' and documentation. The situation is critical.

We stay on the lookout. Hours later, once night has fallen, someone knocks softly at the door.

'Who is it?'

'Pepe Luis.'

Pepe Luis Fernández Albert was a naval officer and member of the aristocracy. Grandson of a general who died in some war or other, whose mother was one of the Spanish queen's protégés.[7] The black sheep of the family, he married a working-class girl and became a communist militant.

A highly cultured man who unreservedly offers his knowledge in the service of the cause, scrupulously honest, Pepe is very down-to-earth, and with a great deal of tact and affection when it comes to the comrades. Everybody loves him. What's funny is that, despite his total simplicity, he is still an aristocrat through and through. He calls you *dear* as if he were meeting you in a salon, bowing deferentially to let you to pass, and he's right to. Because, after all, is it necessary to be refined and polite only with the 'upper class', and coarse with the 'lower-class' wretches? Quite frankly, the attitude of these well-to-do boys to 'act like the proletariat' is not very nice – in fact, it's reactionary, although they believe the opposite – feeling they have to spout all manner of profanities and go around in a filthy state, as if the proletariat – and this is what they believe deep down – were a band of foul-mouthed ragamuffins.

Pepe's entrance is triumphant. When we see him – normally so distinguished looking – unshaven, scratched, dirty and in tatters, our first reaction is to laugh.

And he laughs too. He knows very well it is our bashful way of expressing the great joy we feel at seeing him safe and sound.

Once the laughter has died down, the serious business begins. In other circumstances, they would have told me to get the hell out of there, but they couldn't throw me out of my own house. So, as if I too were part of Guerrilla Command, I listen in, with great interest!

Pepe Luis was in Roullens giving a course on military tactics. When the gendarmes suddenly showed up at the *chantier*, Prats, who had no papers, walked away with a bundle of wood on his back. The gendarmes called after him in vain.

'Hep, l'ami!' (*Hey, pal!*)

'He mustn't have heard you, he's deaf as a post,' one of the guerrillas said.

Then, Pepe Luis, who did have his papers in order, and had the same build as Prats, put on the other man's clothes and beret and very calmly went over to introduce himself, apologising:

'I've been told you were calling me.'

'You're under arrest.'

The others, hidden, looked on. They had to do something to prevent Pepe Luis from being captured.

'Hands up, damn it…!' shouted an Andalusian from behind the bushes.

'Qu'est-ce qu'il dit?' (*What's he saying?*)

A burst from a machine gun answered the question. The *guignols* (gendarmes) – feet don't fail me now! – took off running as fast as they could, leaving the prisoner behind. The guerrillas, firing back, scattered through the forest, and, thinking ahead, buried their weapons in a safe place, before retreating towards number 20, Rue Fabre d'Églantine, my home.

It's an unforgettable night. People are knocking on the door every minute. It's the guerrillas arriving back dirty, clothes torn to shreds, covered in scratches, starving and dying of thirst. Every time another one arrives, my heart swells. There is nothing in the world stronger than the sisterhood of those who fight together.

El Maño, quite the comedian, points at the group of poorly shaven men and suddenly says:

'And if the police arrived now, what would you tell them, lass?'

We all burst out laughing. There are eleven of us, packed in like sardines.

Everyone gives their own version of events as they arrive. The commotion was caused by a guerrilla move – an attack on the German truck that had been taking gold from the Salsigne mine – rather badly planned and which failed due to the untimely presence of two gendarmes. One of the guerrillas left his documentation in the hands of the *guignols*. Documentation that – careless error – was actually the legal one. The papers showed that so-and-so worked as a charcoal burner at the *chantier* in Roullens. Roullens, home not only to Guerrilla Command, but also the Spanish guerrillas' military school.

In spite of everything, we're lucky. None of the men have fallen into Nazi hands. The weapons, hidden in the forest, have been recovered. The guerrillas, supplied with new documents, start to file out.

One of the first, Pepe Luis – now washed, clean-shaven and in half-decent clothes – leaves the house with Tere, Panchín's young, fearless partner.

I have to tell you about Tere and Panchín, our lovers. What a beautiful couple they make! She is blonde, with blue eyes that shine like jewels; he, from the Canary Islands, with curly black hair, jet-black eyes and a wonderful smile. We all love them. They are brave, sincere, good companions, and madly in love. So much so that the guerrillas decide to 'marry them' with complete solemnity and they are given five days off as a wedding present. On the second day, they are forced to cancel the leave: the bride has to leave with a suitcase packed with explosives...

Let's continue. My mission is to accompany El Maño to the station. El Maño has the perfect physique for going undercover: innocent pale eyes, measured gestures, soft voice; he looks more like a mystical seminarist than a magnificent guerrilla leader. A refined, sensitive man, he explains, persuades, never needlessly risks the life of a comrade through carelessness, never raises his voice. And he has such authority!

That morning we set out on the dangerous journey. Arm in arm, like two lovers, we gaze into each other's eyes whenever somebody walks past, hiding Antonio's face. The truth is, instead of sweet nothings, El Maño whispers a string of very funny jokes in my ear. I laugh. It's not that I am particularly brave by nature, but one of El Maño's best qualities is an astonishing serenity that means he is able to take the drama out of the most difficult situations. There is no fear when you are by his side. The most difficult part of the mission remains: getting inside the station. The Gestapo and French *Milice* will no doubt have it under close watch, never mind the fact that Antonio's photograph has fallen into their hands.

Squeezed together tightly, looking into one another's eyes, stroking each other's faces, we pass by casually without looking at anyone, go through the entrance and head straight towards the train, which is about to leave. Nobody has said a word to us. The stationmaster's whistle blows. And at that precise moment I make a blunder. Forgetting my role as lover, I reach out my hand to El Maño in a show of camaraderie. A furious whisper: 'Not my hand, my chops!', and we kiss like you see in the movies: Greta Garbo eat your heart out.

I haven't yet left the station when my shoe heel – the one from the marathon – comes off with a *crack*! and I am forced to hop all the way home. The house is empty. The others have disappeared.

So, were the guerrillas a bunch of fools who couldn't do a thing right?

No. I'm talking about men the likes of whom make History, with a capital H. These same men, not far from now, were to be the architects of the liberation of the south of France. Yes, sometimes they get it wrong. And what of it? Only those who never get involved in anything are never wrong. Besides, as I have said before, my house has only ever been meant as a place of refuge in case of problems. I live with them, not in victories, but in hard and humiliating times, as retreats always are.

Many of these men's lives were cut short; they never experienced wrinkles, false teeth, the rusty knees that come with old age.

Ballester has exactly fifteen days left to live.

El Maño – Ángel Fuertes Vidosa – died in a battle against the Civil Guard in Portell, in 1947.

Pepe Luis Fernández Albert was arrested in Madrid, sentenced to death, and pardoned *in extremis*, spent twenty years in prison.

Panchín – Antonio Medina Vega – was executed by firing squad in Madrid in 1946, at the age of twenty-seven. After he'd received the death sentence and all hope was lost, I bumped into Tere one day in Toulouse. I gave her a friendly hug and in a very shaky voice she asked me, 'You know that Panchín…?' 'I know,' I replied in the same tone. I didn't know what else to say. How could I fool such a brave girl? She nodded gracefully, as if to forget her troubles, and smiled: 'I have a little girl who's a ray of sunshine,' she said, putting on a cheerful voice. But I looked into her eyes. Sad, dead eyes, devoid of that joy of living that had made them shine so brightly. Poor, dear girl!

That is the last image I have of her. Tere – Natividad Peribáñez, from Aragon – died at a young age, in exile.

And now, let's talk about the others, about the monsters. About Bach, for example.[8] Music lovers, please don't be alarmed. My Bach is a Gestapo officer in Carcassonne, at a time when the town in Languedoc is well and truly riddled with Nazis, the streets filled with hefty, blond Wehrmacht warriors goose-stepping, triumphantly shrieking 'Heidi, heido, heida!'[9]

Perfectly tailored white jacket, impeccable tie, immaculate shirt, carefully shaven and hair combed neatly, his nails clean and manicured, giving off a discreet aroma of expensive soap, gleaming with cleanliness, flawless from head to toe; this is how Bach presents himself to the detainees. You find yourself facing him after five or six days in a cell, with no means of washing yourself; dirty, creased, ragged. Then, when Bach lays eyes on you he makes a face, as if to say 'Ugh, how disgusting!', doesn't say a word – which is more humiliating than any beating – and sweeps a white, very white scented handkerchief under his nose.

Bach isn't one of those brainless thugs who only knows how to use his fists. Young, intelligent, quite the psychologist, a genius when it comes to interrogations, he plans his sinister work like a chess player moving a piece, not thinking of this move but three or four moves ahead. He asks a few trivial, insignificant questions, and suddenly *bam!* the trap they hadn't seen coming, backing his victim into a corner. Off with their heads!

To tell him a story is too risky. It's best to keep quiet and face him in silence. To give the arrested resistance fighters their due, almost all of them chose the second strategy. So then Bach, casting aside good manners and the guise of a well-bred man, tortures with cold ferocity, searching out the weak point and never hesitates at the moment to kill.

He ties young Cathala to a beam and sets fire to the farmhouse, roasting him alive. He clubs Ballester, finishing him off with a bullet to the skull. I don't know what he did to Almagro, but when we saw him return from the interrogation, we all knew he was mortally wounded.

I admire Ballester and Almagro a great deal. Ballester, in recent times, has been my closest partner in the struggle and, as we travelled together through hills and valleys, I witnessed his great human qualities at first hand. Far from the gloomy revolutionary. Young, happy as a lark, in love with life, with an outstanding sense of humour, coatless even in the dead of winter, content with a hunk of bread for lunch, taking chances, he is always cheerful and full of youthful enthusiasm. A boy who is crystal clear and pure like spring water.

Almagro, small, skinny as a rake, took a bullet in the battle of the Ebro that left him with a slight limp: he's like a little wounded sparrow. But beneath his weak physical appearance lies an iron soul. Arrested while writing a report, he swallowed the paper in front of the Gestapo officer and resolutely refused to give a statement. They got nothing from him. In prison, physically devastated, he has never once complained. He only cares about others. He's the one who keeps us all going.

Mari is a different story: Bach manages to morally destroy him. Gripped by fear, sweating anxiously, hands trembling, Mari blabs, telling all, making up what he doesn't know, sinking deeper and deeper, losing every shred of human dignity. And Bach, observing his handiwork, has a glare of contempt in his eyes that makes my blood boil.

I remember the Mari of before, a smart and kind boy. Ballester said to us: 'In Barcelona he committed an administrative error and was thrown out. But he wants to make amends, he has a burning desire to fight and he's a worthy kid.' We all agree to accept him; more than that, to give him some responsibility. A bit rashly, as it turns out.

I have made the mistake of going to his house to notify him of the arrests made, without first finding out whether he himself has been arrested. I fall squarely into the trap. I try to get out of it by saying, 'I've come to visit my lover.' 'Who?' I give Mari's name. When he comes in, I throw my arms around him. '*Ah, mon chéri!*' But trembling, the '*chéri*' pulls away from me. 'Is she your girlfriend?' Bach asks. 'Oh, no, she was there at the meeting of the outlaws...'

I defend myself as best I can. Denying and denying. No, 'my boyfriend' is lying. He must have got himself mixed up in some shady business, and now he's trying to implicate me out of jealousy. 'You're afraid I'll get together with someone else, is that it? But it's all useless, you know. "*Salaud!* (swine!)"' Mari's lips are quivering, for he knows the '*salaud!*' I yell angrily at him is no act. But at an imperious gesture from Bach, he fearfully stammers again, 'No, it's not true; she used to come with Ballester and the others.'

Bach rejoices. But I learn something that day: making someone witness the spectacle of a coward in action is not the best way to encourage a person with an ounce of shame to talk. It's like holding a mirror up to yourself: 'Here, look where you'll end up if you let yourself go!' The effect is immediate. It happened to me. Bach says: 'Talk. If not, you won't get out of here alive.' And I'm shocked to hear my voice – is it really mine? – reply insolently, 'What do I care?'

'May God forgive us!' my mother would have said. We all stare at one another, and I think, 'here comes the good part'. A shiver runs down my spine, but I hold the man's stare. He, mute with rage, surprised, resentful. And Mari, who at that precise moment covers his face with his forearm, as if he were the one about to receive the first blow!

There is no blow. I never understood it. Does Bach understand the glaring psychological error he has just made? Possibly. With a brutal flick of his hand, as if erasing me forever, he sends me back to the cells. He never did interrogate me.

With that wave of his hand, he sends me to the hell of Ravensbrück.[10]

Could we have foreseen Mari's weakness? Why did he get involved in the first place – we asked ourselves – if he couldn't hold his nerve? That was too simplistic. A human being is far more complicated.

When they took us into the interrogation together, seeing T. pale and anxious filled me with fear. 'Well, let's see if he...' For it's clear that T. is frightened, very frightened.

Two hours later, when we go down to be taken back to prison, the lad looks at me squarely and his gaze is steady, almost jubilant. 'I didn't say a word,' he says through gritted teeth. 'Did they hit you?' He shrugs his shoulders, as if it didn't matter. 'A few slaps.'

T. had been afraid he wouldn't be able to resist. Now he knows he is capable of enduring it, and he is happy. Anyone who has never felt this fear, let them cast the first stone.

Once we're back in the prison – the German barracks, the '*caserne Laperrine*' – a jailer asks for volunteers to sweep the corridor, and Amantegui and I go out. While we're sweeping, Amantegui (who despite his surname, is not Basque, but from Es Castell, that is Menorcan, from San Carlos) abruptly proposes:

'Do you want to escape?'

'Yes.'

'When they transfer us, stick with me.'

My comrade's words fill me with extraordinary elation. To get away, be part of the liberation that's so close now! That's why, when a few days later they take us out under heavy guard as if we were dangerous 'terrorists', herding us into covered trucks, I'm glad. Could we really escape?

THE ROAD TO HELL

At Carcassonne station, Torrades' wife, Panxita Amantegui, and Miralles' brother throw themselves at their relatives, hugging them tightly. The prisoners are dignified and brave, despite their bodies showing the wounds of savage torture. Almagro, the poor lad barely able to stand, takes my arm affectionately as if trying to comfort me.

They put us in a second-class wagon: the windows are boarded up, the compartment doors open, and the Germans, weapons in hand, occupy the corridor opposite us.

Very discreetly, I move towards the compartment my comrades are in and sit down beside Amantegui.

'What do we have to do?'

'Tonight, the train will go through a place where it has to slow right down; it almost stops. At that point we open the window and jump.'

'They'll shoot. They'll chase us.'

'There's a wood. Beside it a maquis. They'll help us. What do you say?'

I don't give it much thought.

'Okay.'

A German appears at the door to the compartment.

'What are you doing here? Come on, get back with the women! *Raus!*'

'I'll yell,' Amantegui whispers before I leave.

And now I'm in another compartment, full of female prisoners, having to make do with sitting in a space not by the window, but next to the door to the corridor, which is a serious drawback. The escape plan becomes complicated.

I take off my high-heeled shoes and swap them for a pair of sturdy espadrilles. Despite the heat, I keep on my sweater and coat. They might cushion the fall. It's hellishly hot in the compartment, and the other women must think I'm rather crazy.

Needless to say, I don't close my eyes all night. But Amantegui never gave the shout.

At dawn, I cautiously step out into the corridor, without a word from the Germans, and take a look into my comrades' compartment. They're all there.

Amantegui comes out.

'We couldn't do it. The train didn't slow down when we reached the designated spot. We would have been smashed to smithereens. But don't worry. We'll find another opportunity.'

Hugely dejected, I return to the other women. Another opportunity! How on earth do we find it?

A few hours pass. We are close to Orléans. It's hot. It's 6 June 1944 and we are yet to learn that the allies have landed in Normandy.

Suddenly the train stops dead, so abruptly that people, packages and suitcases go flying, and we hear planes overhead, skimming the roof of the train, spitting out a stream of bullets that shatter the windows, causing indescribable panic. Before I realise what's actually happening, I find myself beneath a heap of frightened, screaming women. I finally manage to get out of there and once in the corridor, Mascaró and I try to get out of the train.

Too late. A young German, who hasn't even started shaving, stares at us with the cold gaze of an assassin, aiming his pistol at us.

'*Halt!*'

One thing is very clear. That brat, probably a '*Hitlerjugend*' (Hitler Youth) fanatic, wouldn't think twice about riddling us with bullets. We stop.

Almagro comes out into the corridor, and just as he's getting close to me the planes come again with another whistle of bullets. We all throw ourselves to the ground.

'Amantegui,' he whispers in my ear, 'has escaped out of the window.'

The window! We should have gone for the window. Fool! A thousand times a fool! Amantegui hadn't lost sight of the goal. I could kick myself.

Once the danger was over, the Germans made us file off the train, lined us up, two by two, and counted us.

'There's one missing. Tell us who it is. If you don't, you'll be punished.'

Somebody starts to say:

'He's Spanish, a man with glasses, greyish hair and a beret...'

Without letting him finish, a group of us Spaniards interrupt him:

'We saw a man fitting that description among the wounded they were carrying away...'

Everyone 'had seen him', wounded, maybe even dead... We say it with such conviction that we almost believe it ourselves.

I don't know if the Germans are foolish enough to believe it, or if they don't really want to look for him, but the trick works. They don't move. This buys our comrade some time.

Out of the corner of our eyes, we look around us. A flat expanse of land, without a single tree. Where on earth has Amantegui gone?

Amantegui had simply hidden in a haystack. During the day he must have pulled out a bundle of straw, covered himself with it and held it in place with his hands. At sunset he realised he would have to make a decision. And since he's strong-minded and good at gaining people's trust, he went to a nearby farmhouse and simply knocked on the door.

'Do you know if there are any Spaniards nearby?'

The people in the farmhouse looked him up and down.

'Are you the man who escaped?'

'The very same.'

'Come in.'

His heart swelled at the kindness the family showed him.

'You can't stay here,' they told him. 'This whole area will be thoroughly searched. We'll give you food and you can "steal" the bicycle that's out on the porch. Do you understand? If you're unlucky and are arrested, we'll say it was stolen. Go to our friends' house. They are good French people and will help you. It's 80 kilometres from here. And beware! All the bridges are guarded by the "*frisés*" (Germans)'.

So here's our hero, now a champion cyclist through no choice of his own, the itinerary etched on his brain, at times riding the 'stolen' bicycle, other times carrying it on his back as he wades through water to avoid a bridge.

He reaches the place and is welcomed with open arms at the house. They are members of the resistance. After the initial explanations, they raise the crucial question:

'And now what are you thinking of doing? If you like, we can hide you...'

'I don't want to hide!' protests the man from Es Castell. 'Aren't there any maquis around here?'

Yes, there is one. So, they leave him alone in a room while they go to look for a comrade to take him to the maquis. Our man is overjoyed.

'Suddenly,' – this is Amantegui speaking – 'the door opens and what do I see? The owner of the house and a gendarme. "The wretch has shopped me!" I think. I had no weapon, nothing to hand with which to defend myself. Seeing my face, the two of them start to roar with laughter. The gendarme – a real gendarme, yes indeed! – was a resistance fighter...'

And that's how, the next day, bold as brass, pedalling away happily on the famous 'stolen' bicycle alongside a genuine gendarme, the hero of Es Castell set out for the maquis.

He fought there courageously. He was lucky, and one day a short while after the liberation, dressed in the glorious uniform of the *francs-tireurs*,[11] he called in at the modest apartment on the Rue de l'Hospice in Carcassonne, where Panxita, who adored her man even though he was a bit of a womaniser, and had wept for him, thinking him dead, almost fainted with joy seeing him arrive alive and well.

Someone recently told me that Amantegui lives in Cuba, where he played an active part in the revolution. I can well believe it. It's easy to picture him with a heavy beard in the Sierra Maestra. It would suit him down to the ground.

In Paris, they separate me from my companions. We briefly clutch hands, wishing each other luck. When it's his turn, Almagro, who had been sitting on the ground, doesn't have the strength to stand up. He is physically exhausted. He fixes his blue eyes on me and says, 'Paquita, we have to escape, one way or another.' It's both a farewell and a call to arms.

ROMAINVILLE (OUTSKIRTS OF PARIS, FRANCE)

All of us women are taken to Fort Romainville.[12] The wheels are slowly turning that will take us to the death camps.

At Romainville, as well as a good many French women, I meet two Spaniards: María and Constanza.

Constanza, a refugee and typical *Madrileña*, is a serious, very aware girl, who inspires total confidence. In prison, she began an affair with a prisoner, a Catalan boy, whom she affectionately calls 'my Scrubbing Brush', alluding to her Romeo's hair, clumsily shorn by the guards. She talks about him day and night, with the emotion of a first love. After the liberation of the camps, they married and have been a solid couple ever since. Even today, despite their grey hair, they remain faithful to the ideals they held at twenty.

María is audacious, to the extreme. She used to tell the story, very pleased with herself, of how when she joined the French guerrilla groups, they asked her to get hold of a bicycle, an essential piece of equipment for a new contact: she wandered around a market and saw three bicycles together. 'Why take just one?' she said to herself. And without giving it much thought, she got on one of the bicycles and loaded the other two onto her back. The plan nearly failed, and she was almost caught. Luckily, her comrades arrived in time.

The inmates of Fort Romainville are fairly varied: as well as the seasoned proletarian militants, active participants in every battle, there are peasant women whom the Germans suspect – and rightly so – of having helped the maquis, clerks who supplied documentation or ration cards to the resistance; as well as women from the *haute bourgeoisie* and even the aristocracy – oh yes, a countess, no less – arrested for their Gaullist activities or as hostages, because they had a husband or son in London with General de Gaulle. Of course, all this diversity leads to serious clashes. However, class differences aside, we are united by a common hatred of the Nazi occupiers.

They are still treating us with a modicum of decency. They let us go outside every day. We are often given packages from the Quakers and the Red Cross.[13] And needless to say, those prisoners of the highest social status receive a good deal of food, clothing and money from their relatives. Not only do they eat properly and dress elegantly, but they also have the resources to pay for a servant, that is, a prisoner who washes their clothes and carries out all their tasks in exchange for money. They are the high-ranking prisoners.

All these women from rich families are convinced that the Germans respect them. 'They would never dare do anything to me. *J'ai beaucoup de relations…*'. And they talk about the Geneva Convention here, and human rights there… It won't be long before they lose these illusions.

Please don't think I am laughing at them. Those women behaved very decently when times got hard later on and, despite our differences, we formed a solid wall that our enemies often crashed into.

'Paquita, we have to escape.' We do, but how? I sniff around everywhere. 'Has nobody ever escaped from here?' My question raises smiles. Escape from Romainville?

It's not straightforward. And, even if I did manage it, where would I go in Paris, totally alien to me?

I talk about it with Germaine, a good friend. 'Go to Aubervilliers, number 12, Rue Albinet. The whole neighbourhood will help you,' she says simply.

There's just one key element missing: getting out of Romainville.

The communal toilets consist of a large hole that leads into pipework large enough for a person to fit inside. It would be a tight squeeze, but I'm not too big and am fairly agile. Might it be possible to escape this way? Where could the pipe lead to? The Seine, presumably. Appearing in the middle of Paris in broad daylight covered head to toe in excrement, asking for directions to Rue Albinet in Aubervilliers... Who knows? Maybe the sewer workers I come across could help me, given that the underground network of sewers has the same name as the corresponding streets above. I need to do some research.

The following day I find myself by the toilets when the siren sounds. An air raid. They happen often now.

Instead of going into the building, where they lock us during the alarms, I stay in the latrines, determined to try my luck. Once alone, having time at my disposal – the alarms go on for a long while – I study the hole closely. Suddenly a torrent of hundreds of litres of water gushes down, under enormous pressure. The Nazis have foreseen everything. The same thing happens at regular intervals. If I had got into the pipe, I would have drowned. I shudder with retrospective fear. I'm forced to admit defeat.

At that precise moment, a German guard arrives and starts screaming like a madwoman as soon as she sees me. She pushes me forward, forcing me up some stairs and locks me in a little attic, with a single window protected by a thick grille. I am kept there for over two hours, raging.

Finally, the same guard opens the door and rattles off something in German, which is clearly quite threatening, but which I don't understand a scrap of, and makes me go down to the communal dormitory.

My arrival causes quite a sensation: the prisoners thought I had escaped. They had all noticed my absence, as one of them had found the round tin plate with my prisoner number on it next to the main door; it had probably fallen off when the *fräulein* had jostled me. 'How daring!' – they said admiringly – 'Not only has she escaped, but she's left them the plate to rub their noses in it...'

Word had spread and they had all decided to keep quiet and cover up my escape as best they could to give me a little time.

But in the end, the heroine, the Montecristo in a skirt, had turned out to be a poor crackpot who came off looking a fool.

The adventure was comical and my role in it not particularly elegant, but it gave me a valuable insight into the solidarity of those women. Bearing in mind that the Germans are quick to dole out terrible collective punishments when it comes to escape attempts, the gesture was beautiful and one I couldn't underestimate. I'm so very grateful.

We don't stay at Romainville for long. One day, a German reads out a list and – come on! – everyone onto the trucks, well-guarded by a group of thugs from Mussolini's OVRA[14] – black sideburns, the brim of their hats over their eyes, black shirts and flashy ties – looking like something out of a gangster movie, one of those starring George Raft in the 1930s. No chance of escaping. They know their role.

Some years later, I learned that despite everything there was one prisoner who escaped Romainville: the legendary Colonel Fabien, a seventeen-year-old volunteer in the International Brigades.[15] He was never caught.

SAARBRÜCKEN (GERMANY)

At Saarbrücken, all I see is one street, one long endless street and a row of women, us, walking in pairs towards the concentration camp. Were there houses, trees, people? I don't know. Any peripheral vision has been erased from my memory. Perhaps I looked nowhere but straight ahead, so as not to see the SS officers on either side, pistols in hand, their splendid boots click-clacking on the fine ash, repeating their strident cries of *Schnell, schnell!*; a litany that would soon become all too familiar.[16]

They still call us by our names; we're still wearing our own clothes, some stepping out in *haute couture*, others more simply dressed. And us, the Spanish refugees, on the bottom rung of the scale of elegance. We had fled into exile with only the clothes on our backs, and were able to make some rudimentary alterations, so that with a lot of skill and darning we manage – thank goodness – to protect our modesty.

We don't know where they are taking us, but we do know the Greater Reich aren't sending us on holiday.[17] Some are hopeful. Not so, we Spaniards. We're already familiar with fascism.

The SS guards, screaming like lunatics, arrange us in rows. From the moment we set foot in Saarbrücken, our captors' attitude has changed dramatically. In Romainville, they spoke to us properly. When we left the fort, they had even gone to the trouble of giving each of us a wonderful food parcel from the Red Cross and transporting us in a half-decent passenger wagon. Whenever they spoke to us, they did so either in basic French, or tried to find a translator. Here they scream at us, in German. Their tone of voice is incredibly brutal, and their demeanour, pistol in hand, constantly threatening. At Saarbrücken, good manners are a thing of the past.

At the office by the gate, which we are made to enter one by one, the looting begins. The SS officers, male and female alike, fight over the prisoners' clothing, jewellery, furs, purses; behaving like animals, guffawing as they shamelessly scoff the contents of the torn Red Cross parcels we had so ostentatiously been given.

The sophisticated Madame V. leaves the office with a face like a beetroot, her eyes flashing with rage.

'Thieves! They plundered me horribly. Two of those beastly women wanted my shawl; they were pulling it from either side, so I had to take it off myself before they strangled me with it. A hand-embroidered shawl I bought in Egypt.'

Beside me, Madame S. starts to fret:

'They won't take my gold rosary from me. They'll respect that. Because the Geneva Convention...'

To hell with the Geneva Convention!

'They're Nazis,' I tell her, sceptically. 'And surely you know the Nazis wipe their boots on the Geneva Convention. Can't you see that?'

Beginning to have her doubts, Madame S. hides the rosary in a fold of the beautiful hat she's wearing. Unfortunately, a stocky SS *fräulein* takes a fancy to the hat, and quickly snatches it from her.

Pillaged and indignant, following a guttural command, we shuffle forward a few steps and line up in rows, *'fünf und fünf*, five by five.

Suddenly we are struck dumb with indescribable terror: drifting toward us from every direction are human beings who look like ghosts, the very image of death: as transparent as larvae, with faces like skulls, all teeth and eyes, skeletal bodies, fleshless hands of the dead, heads shaved to the scalp, dressed in rags. The prisoners.

There is a deathly silence. Frozen by fear, for the very first time we grasp the answer to a question that has always tormented us: What do the Nazis do with their prisoners? After arrest, resistance fighters disappeared without a trace. Never to be heard of again. Family and comrades would never know where they ended up. *Nacht und Nebel* – Night and Fog![18] The horrifying answer was finally given to us by those wretched prisoners in Saarbrücken concentration camp, one of so many in Nazi Germany.

Their pale faces are etched with profound, intense pain, like nothing I could have imagined in a human being; the pain of extreme hunger, mortal exhaustion, torture, beatings, of ravaged dignity. And despite everything – a miracle of being convinced they have fought for what is right – in their eyes shines a light that makes them infinitely superior to their executioners, a tiny light that seems to say, 'even here a person can retain their humanity'.

The SS officers, blond, healthy, ruddy-cheeked, well-fed, smartly dressed, spotlessly clean, look at them and then at us, back and forth, laughing grotesquely, relishing our terror.

We feel a mixture of pity, pain, indignation and dark foreboding. The Nazis will soon turn us into fleshless Dantean ghosts too. We imagined we'd be locked up in a fort, shot, God knows what else, but not this. This surpasses every horror imaginable.

Two young French women, not long interned in the camp judging by their appearance – less exhausted than the rest of their comrades – come over and give us a friendly wave. We smile back at them. An SS guard immediately barks an order, and the girls start to run round the swimming pool. (Only afterwards, following the Nazis' fall, will the world come to know the horrifying truth: many prisoners were ruthlessly, deliberately drowned there by the Nazis).

At first, we don't pay much attention to this little race, we assume it's exercise. Only when we notice their pained expressions do we begin to understand. Worn out, their pace begins to falter. And whenever this happens, an SS officer appears, takes out his pistol and forces them to run, to keep running, on and on. *Schnell!* It's not a joke, and it's not some punishment for naughty schoolgirls.

Other officers push another three prisoners forward, Soviet women. They punish them for every tiny slip, perhaps just to make an 'example' of them, the sadistic pleasure of seeing us suffer. Or perhaps for their own entertainment. I don't know. I find it impossible to get inside the mind of an SS guard, it is and always will be a mystery to me.

Another bark and the three Soviet women start to run round the swimming pool too, squatting, with their hands behind their heads and barefoot. The position, difficult even for a person in good health, was like torture for those exhausted prisoners.

Biting their lips, the three Soviet women struggle desperately. Each time their trembling legs lose their rhythm the SS officers are upon them, screaming savagely, waving their pistols, viciously stamping on their victims' feet with their well-polished heavy boots. Tears and mucus cover the wretched women's faces and on their feet the blood combines with the fine ash that covers the avenues around the camp. All the while, stumbling and exhausted, the French women continue to run round the swimming pool. *Schnell!*

Nobody ever mentioned the Geneva Convention again after that.

The routine at Saarbrücken is the same every day for the eight days we are there. In the morning, they take us to the 'showers': a dirty, ominous room with a few taps. The first day we start to undress. But three seconds later, shouting and pushing, they usher us out, without even letting us put our clothes back on. We have to do this outside, the SS guards sniggering as they watch. Every day it's the same. We don't even undress now, we just wash our hands and faces, not even really able to do that. How can we, in a matter of seconds, with more than twenty women to each tap? We become gradually dirtier, a humiliation we feel keenly.

From the 'showers', we go to the canteen: a room with an endless table in the middle, rough benches either side, where we are forced to sit, without moving, silent and with our hands on the table, for hours on end.

At midday, nettle soup boiled with water and salt. One tiny scrap of bread each. Nothing more. And once again silence and no moving. Until, without supper of course – the nettles being the only 'meal' of the day – we go to the dormitory. There we have to lie on narrow, hard sleeping mats laid on triple bunks made of rough planks. The distance between each bed is so small that it is like sleeping in a burial niche. We sleep there unbelievably crammed in; and since the doors and windows are hermetically sealed from the outside, the air soon becomes unbreathable. Gasping for breath, on the verge of asphyxiating, we feel our temples might explode.

After eight days of this routine, we are taken out of Saarbrücken. They give us each a hunk of bread and as I recall a scrape of margarine and a few slices of sausage. Nothing else.

Without getting too close, the miserable Saarbrücken prisoners furtively wave their farewells. An old woman – a good woman, full of compassion – is unable to stop herself, and tosses her bread to a prisoner, a spectre with a pained expression, frightening to behold. An SS officer notices, and before the hungry prisoner can get his hands on the bread he catches it, throws it to the ground and stamps on it with his well-shined boots. Afterwards he gestures as if to say: 'Eat it now, if you like.' But the little Soviet lad doesn't stoop to pick up the crumbs of bread mixed with ash.

We had travelled from Romainville in a passenger wagon. In Saarbrücken, they put us in cattle wagons. To breathe, we have a tiny window which they have taken pains to cover with barbed wire. On the journey a large drum (without a lid, that goes without saying) serves as a privy for the whole wagon – fifty-three women. Once we're all inside, they close the wagon and seal the doors.

Saarbrücken station is crowded with people who watch indifferently as we go by. Seeing ourselves penned up like animals fills us with rage. We have to do something. To shout, loud and strong, about who we are – women of the resistance. I don't know which wagon leads the way. I think it was ours. With fury, with rage, at the top of our voices, we start to sing 'La Marseillaise'. The chorus spreads to every wagon, strident and powerful. The verses of the anthem of the French Revolution burst forth in defiance to the station hung with swastikas.

> *Marchons, marchons*
> *Qu'un sang impur*
> *Abreuve nos sillons!*

Never again have I heard a 'Marseillaise' quite like it. Nobody has ever sung the hymn of the '*sans-culottes*' with more strength and conviction than we did in that coal-mining city. The 'Marseillaise' we sang that day was a far cry from the solemn, pompous, funereal hymn you hear nowadays at official ceremonies!

An unbearable stench soon spreads throughout that ghastly wagon – the smell of urine and excrement, the sweat of women who haven't washed in eight days. Five days, in almost total darkness, breathing in filth, dirty, hungry. Five days during which we received no more supplies, nor even a drop of water. Did they intend for us to die of thirst? Luckily, one of the women, a young blonde girl from Alsace – I believe her name was Huguette – has managed, I don't know how, to get hold of a little half-litre bottle. Every time the train stops, Huguette carefully reaches her slim, white arm through the window wire, shaking the bottle and calling out in German:

'*Wasser, bitte!*' (Water, please!)

Who are the people who fill the bottle: railway workers, soldiers, travellers, women? I don't know. All I can say is that every time the bottle is handed back full, and every time Huguette's arms are covered with new, cruel scratches.

With absolute discipline, we take turns to share the scarce water equally. Nobody complains. Nobody tries to take advantage, increasing their share to the detriment of others. It's very little, but that sip of water swallowed from time to time allows us to reach Ravensbrück alive.

I shudder to think what would have happened should that bottle of water have fallen into the hands of an SS guard, or any other swastika fanatic. Any chance of survival would have been thwarted.

The fact that someone carried out that humane act in every station underlined something: not all Germans were Nazis. Hope wasn't yet dead and buried.

RAVENSBRÜCK (GERMANY)

Thirsty, hungry, filthy, dizzy from lack of air, exhausted, many of us sick, after those five days it is horrific to recall, we are met at Fürstenberg station by a large contingent of vociferous SS officers, accompanied by enormous police dogs growling and baring their teeth. Woe betide anyone who puts a step out of line!

This rabble leads us on foot to Ravensbrück concentration camp. There are sick women, some crippled, old women in their eighties who can barely keep up.

Along the way we see quaint little houses with starched floral curtains, blonde children with cheeks as rosy as apples, so many children, playing in the grass strewn with small, brightly coloured flowers; a pleasant, charming life, that for us, destined for Hell, is now no more than a mirage.

What dreadful irony! Those happy little houses are the homes of our executioners, the SS of the camp; those children, the monsters' sons and daughters; and the flowers owe their beauty to a special fertilizer: the ashes of the prisoners incinerated in the crematorium.

Do you know what it means to stand in line for twelve hours, forbidden to move a hand or foot? After five days' travelling, locked in stinking cattle wagons, tortured by a thirst that sets your throat on fire, starving, delirious from lack of sleep, and now in the middle of the night struggling to stand against a freezing wind.

This, then, is the welcome – a fitting prologue to what awaits us – that we receive at Ravensbrück concentration camp.

We arrive crushed with exhaustion, dreaming with our eyes open: oh, for a glass of water, a cup of hot soup, even if only made with nettles, any old pallet upon which to rest our stiff bodies!

We didn't have much hope: we assumed we wouldn't be able to wash, that the soup would be bad and the water, who knows, perhaps murky, the bed as hard as stone. But what we could not yet imagine, because it was beyond our comprehension, were those twelve hours – from five in the afternoon to five in the morning – spent standing in rows, surrounded by threatening cracks of the whip and incomprehensible shouting.

And next to the SS men and women, scolding us, shoving us violently, the *Kapos*,[19] *Blockovas*[20] and *Stubovas*[21] paced back and forth, making up a kind of moth-eaten aristocracy of the camp. Generally common law prisoners, they effectively help the SS in exchange for certain wretched privileges. They carry out the repression ruthlessly, telling their owners everything the prisoners do and say, throwing punches and beatings everywhere, yelling and cruelly insulting us.

Upon our arrival, seeing them in the wide grey and navy blue vertically striped prison uniforms, we believed in good faith that they were worthy companions in misfortune. We soon realised our mistake: the *kapos* were just as dangerous an enemy as the Nazis themselves.

At five o'clock in the morning, the *kapos* bark a few words in an unknown language and unceremoniously push us forward, still in our rows. We all cheer up. At last!

'Look,' a woman points. 'Down there are the kitchens. See the smoke coming out of the chimney?'

It was the crematorium.

Shouting and pushing ensues, barked orders in a language we don't understand, and we are on our way to what we believe are the showers. Finally, we can wash and have a drink!

The scene that awaits us is a little different. We're made to enter in small groups, while the rest queue outside. Observing us with disgusted expressions, a few female SS officers surrounded by *kapos* force us to strip completely naked. They take everything, absolutely everything from us, even handkerchiefs and sanitary towels. We're left as naked as when our mothers brought us into the world. Whenever they feel like it, they subject a prisoner to an intimate search. Then they meticulously examine our hair, armpits, pubic area, in search of hypothetical parasites. It is undignified, humiliating. One peasant woman has splendid blonde hair – they roughly chop it all off at her scalp with scissors, as if shearing an animal. Methodical economists of crime, the Nazis use victims' hair to make fabric.

We are shoved roughly under the showers. The water is freezing. They don't give us soap or towels. Too much of a luxury. Thirsty, we eagerly swallow the drops of water that splash on our faces. A few seconds later, more shouting and pushing. Now, totally drenched with cold water, they usher us towards the door. SS officers and *kapos* await us with four colossal wicker baskets. Shirts in one, the kind our great-grandmothers used to wear, once white; in another, badly laundered knickers with large stains in the crotch; in the third basket, huge boots, size forty and above, falling apart and without laces; and, in the last one, dresses of all colours and sizes, all filthy and faded, with one common feature: an enormous red painted cross, like a huge multiplication sign, front and back.

No point trying to choose. If anyone attempts to find a dress their size or points out that they've been given two shoes for the same foot, the response is immediate: a push or a kick where it hurts the most. *Raus, schnell*! And back outside.

A French woman stops:

'At least give me a sanitary towel. I'm menstruating!'

The woman gets a kick and, blood dripping down her legs, is forced to leave with the others.

I get a horrible dress with red and blue stripes, like a mattress, ancient, dirty, faded and which judging by its size, seems to have been made for a giantess. It comes right down to my feet. Constanza emerges looking much the same. And how we laugh!

'Constanza, you look like a tramp.'

'And you look like a rag and bone woman, my dear...'

Madame V., the one with the Egyptian shawl, appears shorn, with a ragged, grubby dress and tattered shoes. For a moment I fear she's going to burst into tears. But no. She spins around, pinching her skirt with her fingertips, saying:

'Feast your eyes on the *haute couture* design...'

Everyone goes out. Some livid, others laughing their heads off. Nobody weeps. Even the grandmothers – there are four or five in their eighties – take it in their stride. They can't humiliate those they want to, only those they can.

In our disguises, we go one by one into an office. Behind the desk sits a prisoner – French and political, according to the red triangle with the letter F on her zebra uniform – a woman with grey hair and clear, intelligent, shining eyes. She interrogates me.

'Spanish?'

'Yes.'

'Arrested where?'

'In France.'

A questioning look.

'Political refugee.'

She looks at me and casts her eyes down to the papers. Then, in a very weak voice, without looking at me, she says:

'I know Spain. Albacete.'

Albacete! The International Brigades. My heart pounds with a rush of emotion. She looks up and our eyes meet. A click. A smile. We have understood one another.

Silence. And then, in a low voice:

'Are you sick?'

'No.'

'If any of you are sick, don't mention it.'

Surprised, I open my mouth to ask why. But the French woman silences me with a wave of her hand.

'Tell the others.'

'I will.'

A farewell gesture, a slight smile; and in Spanish, with the "r" caught at the back of her throat:

'*No pasarán!*'

'Ah, no, now they definitely shall not pass.'

Something she said plays on my mind. What had the comrade meant when she told me that under no circumstances should we say we were unwell?

Some French women confirm the report:

'Yes. A French prisoner, a political prisoner, told us the same thing.'

They don't understand the meaning of the warning either. But just in case, we decide to follow the advice to the letter.

Shouting, shoving and new barked orders in who knows what language by the SS pack of hounds and the *kapos*; into rows of five again – *Fünf und fünf!* they roar at us – and we are taken to a hut.

They add a few hundred Polish and Soviet women, as well as some Jews. There are children among the latter: pale, skinny, with huge, terrified adult eyes.

In the barracks, there are only a few basic wooden stools, and not enough for everyone. We rub elbows, knees; the lack of space forces us into total immobility, which becomes extremely painful after half an hour, so imagine what it's like after a whole day! You feel like lashing out at everyone around you. Frayed nerves give rise to some unpleasant incidents.

A good while later, they finally serve us a rather unpleasant soup, but since we are so hungry, we all wolf it down.

Mid-afternoon, I inch my way through this human mass, not without protests, and manage to reach a window. Outside some prisoners, already veterans in the camp, are wandering around our block, trying to garner fresh news. Suddenly I recognise among them Lola García Etxebarrieta, an old fighter and good friend of mine from Barcelona. Without thinking, I jump out of the window. We hug each other tightly.

'I'm called Charlie here,' she whispers.

'And I'm Paquita.'

Lola gets straight to the point:

'Tell me, the second front… and what's happening in Spain?'

I tell her everything I know. She listens attentively. When I finish, it strikes me that it's my turn to ask questions.

'Lola, we've been told that if one of us is sick, we shouldn't tell them. Why is this?'

Lola is a sincere, brave woman. The hand that grips my arm is trembling a little. But she has no choice but tell the truth.

'Some time ago you know, a truck load of women arrived,' she begins. 'They were all Soviet. They arrived at sunset and were lined up outside. It was deepest, darkest winter. The next morning when we went to work, they were still there, standing in rows. Some were on the ground, dead, maybe passed out, I don't know. It was forbidden to touch them. When we returned from work at night, the women were still in the same place, motionless, but naked. The next morning almost all of them were dead. But a few wretches remained there, still standing. Those eyes…! When we came back from work, the square was empty. Are you beginning to understand what kind of place Ravensbrück is?'

'Can it be true, Lola?'

With a wave of her hand, she points to two girls.

'Look at their legs.'

The girls' legs have two long and very deep scars running down them.

'What is that?'

'Scientific experiments by Nazi doctors. Their bone marrow has been removed. They're the guinea pigs of block 32. Their legs give way all the time. Crippled for life. They do even worse things to others. Many, practically all of them, die. Or they kill them, to study the effects of the "scientific" experiments on their bodies.'

Lola carries on, and she tells me everything, absolutely everything, with the sincerity one has with a fellow fighter to whom one can tell the truth, even if it is terrifying. And I don't know what to say in response, I can't find a single word. All the horror of Ravensbrück has just hit me, like a bucket of cold water.

I won't say any more about you, Lola. A few years after we returned to France, a small news item in a Paris newspaper said you and your husband, Quimet Olaso, had died of gas poisoning in your flat. Accident? Suicide? I heard that some had criticised Olaso for having shown weakness when he faced the Gestapo. Was that true, and you couldn't bear the shame? Or perhaps it was simply a bout of depression, from the suffering of being deported? The death camps kill from afar as well.

That night I can't sleep. Lola has told me such horrors! When, exhausted, my eyes finally close, an insistent image haunts me like a nightmare:

When I was little, a dog cart often passed through the neighbourhood. A chorus of barks, growls, moans. The women and children used to look scathingly at the men driving the cart:

'Bunch of layabouts, why don't you actually work instead of chasing those poor dogs!'

Once, in the Plaza del Pino, in Barcelona, the men with the dog cart caught a young, pure white pup. When they lassoed him, he let out a tiny, high-pitched cry, like a child. I shuddered. I felt so sorry for him it made me want to cry.

'Poor things, they kill them with gas,' said a woman beside me.

I couldn't sleep that night either.

It must be awful to die by being gassed...

Appell! Appell! Schnell![22]

The loudspeakers blare out something in German and repeat it in Polish. What did it say? We all wonder, dazed, waiting in vain for a translation. But the *blockova* and *stubovas*, yelling and pushing us towards the door with threatening, powerful shoves, force us out of the hut.

Without fully understanding, we come out into a large square in front of the barracks and see thousands of prisoners lining up in rows. The *kapos*, *blockovas* and other officials examine the rows meticulously. Not a shoulder, head or foot can break the impeccable straight line. Turning your head, moving a foot or a hand, making the most insignificant movement, is immediately sanctioned with shoving and slapping. And the women are no slouches!

We rookies don't manage to form neat rows. The whole pack yells at us, pushing us brutally, slapping and hitting us with sticks left, right and centre.

Eventually, after considerable effort, they get the entire camp to form perfect rows, completely motionless and maintaining absolute silence. The slightest movement, a mere whisper is punished immediately with beatings.

Appell! Appell! Doesn't only refer to the physically unbearable posture, the exhaustion, the hours of cold, but also the total dehumanisation, the feeling of not being a living being, but merely a number, an object. Neither hunger, nor the lashes, nor the perpetual threat of the gas chamber reach as deep into your soul as the profound humiliation of seeing yourself forced to command your own muscles to a stony immobility, to fix a passive expression on your face, not to flinch, even when the blow falls on the martyred flesh of a comrade, friend, sister.

You feel defeated, a coward, as if in one fell swoop, they have stripped you of your dignity as a fighter; you feel disgusted and ashamed of yourself. However hard I try; I'll never be able to fully describe what the *appell* is.

I remember having been to see *Stronger than the Night* at the cinema, a film made by German anti-fascists. In a concentration camp, a group of German prisoners perform a roll call. At a certain point, one of them slightly moves his head. I was terrified and my heart pounded violently.

'What's the matter?' said someone beside me, when the SS whip lashed the prisoner. I had 'found' myself back at the *appell*. Recoiling, I had foreseen the Nazi whip and, unconsciously, I adopted the stillness of a statue, the expressionless face of the deportees during roll call, and felt that same deep shame.

I left the cinema and didn't even know where I was going. For several days afterwards, I experienced sudden memory lapses, a wound all deportees inherit from the camps and one we carry around with us for the rest of our lives. I'm not telling you to garner pity. I'm telling you so you understand just how deep a wound – as if seared with a branding iron – the *appell* left us with.

Raus, raus, Schnell!

Now what do they want? Shouts, shoves, the whole repertoire. By dint of all the shouting and slapping, we are beginning to understand German. The prospect of a whipping and the spectre of the gas chamber are far more effective than all the Berlitz methods in the world.

This time we have to go out completely naked. Some elderly women desperately try to keep their underwear on, but the *kapos* viciously rip them off.

Once again, we're lined up in the square and there we stand, stock still, for an eternity. The grandmothers among us feel shame at seeing their ageing, unsightly bodies exposed in this way and hold back their tears with dignity. They are a sorry sight. It's so hard to see yourself like this, cruelly mocked at the end of a beautiful, pure life.

Groups of SS with dogs in tow roam the area, brandishing their pistols. Personally, I feel no shame in seeing myself naked in their presence, as if I was just another dog, or a boulder. After seeing them day after day, barking insults and lashing out like true beasts, I have come to exclude them from the human race. To me, they are bipeds and nothing more.

Another hour of roll call, still naked, until they make us go forward. A little way off an SS officer awaits us, with clear, cold eyes, sitting sprawled beside a table. The scene I describe next takes place in total silence: we have to step forward, one by one, turn around as if trying on a dress at the dressmaker's, tilt your head towards the SS officer and open your mouth. The Nazi notes something down, and that's it. Next! *Schnell!*

'Is he a dentist?' some ask in good faith.

The horrifying truth, which luckily most are unaware of, is that this is the first selection for the gas chamber. The elderly, those with physical defects, mutilations or visible diseases are eliminated. Out! To the gas chamber, the crematorium. The Greater Reich has no interest in feeding useless mouths.

Perfect accountants, they make notes: 'Prisoner X, two gold teeth'. And when prisoner X expires, hollowed out by dysentery, exhausted by starvation and tuberculosis or killed by *Zyklon* gas, the two gold teeth will be recovered.[23] A stamp on the corpse's cheek indicates that the operation has been performed. And then there we are, ready for the crematorium!

In Ravensbrück, it's extremely dangerous to have too many gold teeth. The following afternoon, barking profusely and shoving us, they make us strip again and go out. What more do they want? The inevitable roll call follows, out in the square. Afterwards, always five by five, they make us enter a sinister-looking place.

There is a dirty, stained stretcher of sorts, and next to it the 'doctor', a big giant of a woman with a short, muscular neck, like a fairground wrestler, masculine features and huge hands.

It is quite clear what this is: a gynaecological examination.

If anyone shows the slightest reluctance, the 'doctor' shoves her back on the table and, unceremoniously parting her legs, proceeds with the examination. After around five hundred examinations, the water in the basin, never once changed, is cloudy with pus, blood and all manner of germs.

That examination allows them to send some of the prisoners who have escaped the first inspection by the 'dentist' to be exterminated. Some due to genital diseases or fibroids. Others because they are pregnant.

Yes, the woman who are expecting a child are systematically led to the gas chamber. First, because the Nazis only keep alive those who can work at full capacity, and second, because they don't want children of 'inferior races'. All for the glory and purity of Swastika Germany.

Ravensbrück camp is made up of dozens of large barracks, called 'blocks'. Surrounding the camp, a double row of electric wire fencing, making any escape attempt practically impossible. For even greater security, there are tall watchtowers where guards armed with machine guns survey the entire camp, ready to shoot: not into the air, but to kill without a second thought. And if we add to the presence of the SS guards the many dogs trained in hunting prisoners – their jaws send more than a few to the cemetery, or rather the crematorium; as well as the assistance of the rabble of *kapos* and other degenerates, you'll understand that all our escape plans have very little hope of success. But we have to keep trying. We Spaniards never give up hope of escaping.

We find ourselves in quarantine, that is, locked up in the barracks together with a large group of Polish and Soviet women as well as some Jewish women with young children between the ages of five and ten. During the *appell*, the children have to remain immobile, like us, for hours on end. Frightened by the shouting, pushing and abuse, the little ones have already learned not to move a muscle or cry even when they're hungry, afraid or cold. Do they know what soon awaits them? Can they sense it? Remembering the profound sadness in their eyes, adult eyes that go right through you, I think they did. For us deportees, the memory of those Jewish children is like a permanent wound that never heals. This is why when someone, in their name, has the nerve to justify other genocides, it hurts as if I were seeing them murdered for a second time.

The forced coexistence with women who speak languages we don't know creates a huge problem: how can we understand one another? Because understanding one another is essential: it means the possibility of uniting our efforts, creating indispensable solidarity, taking action when an opportunity arises.

First, as deaf people do, we gesticulate with our hands, eyes, mouth, we point at things and each name them in our own language. Later on come the attempts, not always fruitful, to begin to compose sentences, the aim of which is to achieve basic German: 'eat', 'sleep', 'bread', 'silence'. Little by little, we start to understand a few words in languages we have never heard before. The Polish *proixe panyi* – please ma'am– is quickly adopted by all nationalities, as well as the Russian *nye poiemaiu* – I don't understand you. One curious case, the French expression *comme ci comme ça*, or rather 'more or less', comes to mean 'stealing', and is used in that way by everyone, even the French women themselves. Why? Perhaps because of that expressive hand gesture that means 'more or less', which if exaggerated a little can suggest stealing?

Sometimes we softly sing well-known revolutionary songs – we Spanish know a fair few – smiling at finding common ground.

Having said that, don't believe that our relations were overly idyllic. Clashes happen often, as is almost inevitable between women forced to live together for twenty-four hours a day, in subhuman conditions: hunger, overcrowding, lack of sleep, and the endless struggle with the unsurmountable language barrier that prevents us from making ourselves properly understood. But for the most part, we never came to blows. The SS are a constant reminder that the enemy is Nazism.

After gesticulating wildly and drawing an imaginary map of Europe on a table to show her Spain, I manage to explain to Tassia, from Dnipropetrovsk, that I am Spanish. *Ispanca!* – she shouts excitedly. *Ispanca!* – and hugs me passionately.

'If they ask you what you are, say "*ispancas*",' I tell Constanza and María, very pleased with the discovery.

I don't wait to be asked, but repeat the magic word non-stop, marvelling at its effect. People squeeze my hands, hug me, and some, pronouncing it very badly, even say something along the lines of '*No pasarán*'.

It isn't always plain sailing. One day, I almost get it in the neck. Constanza is asking – in perfect French – the Belgian woman who 'lives' in the bunk above her to please stop wriggling around on the straw mattress, because all the mess ends up falling on her. Constanza believes all Belgians speak French. But the woman is Flemish and doesn't understand a word.

'Constanza,' I butt in, 'it's pointless speaking to her in French. She can't understand you. She's a *flamenca*.'

Oh goodness, what did I say?! The Flemish woman, eyes flashing, yelling, tries to scrabble up to my 'apartment' – the fourth bunk. And it's very clear she's getting ready to punch my lights out.

Constanza is already preparing to defend me, and María, watching the scene from a distance, runs towards us, ready for battle.

Luckily, another Belgian who speaks French and Flemish joins us. She says to me:

'Why did you insult this woman?'

'Who, me?'

'Yes, you. You called her a "*flamenker*". That's a very serious insult.'

We three Spaniards start to laugh, explaining that in Spanish *flamenca* is the direct translation of *vlamish*.

We all laugh and the incident ends here. Every time I meet the Flemish woman in question, we both smile with a knowing look. And to think we weren't far from scratching each other's eyes out!

Oh, and I have to tell you this. Do you know the worst insult a Soviet woman can say? The equivalent of 'son of a...'? Parasite. Nice, isn't it? We learned so much!

One morning, *kapos* and *blockovas* start their shrieking, even louder than usual. The female commandant of Ravensbrück is coming to visit our block in person.

Tall, in a resplendent uniform, her boots creaking, shiny as mirrors, whip in hand and a contemptuous expression on her face, the commandant observes us coldly, one by one, studying us intently.

Suddenly she raises her gloved hand and points her whip at a prisoner. It's a Polish woman, a poor wretch who has lost her mind. She spends hour upon hour cowering in a corner, silent, motionless, an expression of animal terror in her eyes. She's perfectly harmless and we all treat her with affection, assuming her madness is the result of some awful tragedy.

Once the commandant has left, the *kapos* take her away. 'To the infirmary', they tell us when we ask where they're taking her.

A couple of hours later, the Frenchwoman Doctor L.P., goes to the infirmary. She is a very well-balanced woman, full of common sense and courage. But when she returns, she can hardly speak, and the colour has drained from her face.

There is silence. We all look at her, holding our breath.

'They've murdered her', she says in a grave voice. 'I have thoroughly examined the body and there's no doubt. She's been given a lethal injection.'

They have made their selection. On one side the sick, the elderly, the pregnant women. On the other the young, the strong ones, the ones who can be used as slaves. The first group are destined for the *Zyklon* gas. The others are assigned to work in a *kommando*.[24] Constanza, María and I are considered useful.

Devastated, we say goodbye to the 'useless' ones. Do they know what awaits them? Some, perhaps. But if they do suspect it, they have the courage to keep quiet.

They are taking us to the 'pink blocks', they tell us. We won't have to do roll call there.

'The pink blocks!', 'Night and Fog!' The Nazis have mastered the art of hiding their crimes behind poetic phrases.

We 'useful' ones are sent through the showers. Once again, our bodies, already quite emaciated, are meticulously examined for parasites and they give us a light grey short-sleeved uniform, a new coarsely woven shirt and a pair of knickers. In addition, a red triangle (to denote political prisoners) and a number printed in black on a small rectangle of white fabric, which we will have to sew on the sleeve. We keep the huge, tattered boots without laces. Constanza becomes 4,067 and I am 4,068. You have to learn your number in German, because when they call you, if you don't immediately answer, *Ja!*, you get a slap. Needless to say, thanks to this vigorous pedagogic procedure, we all manage to perfectly master the complicated Germanic numerals, and very quickly too!

Before we leave, they line us up in rows near the camp exit. One prisoner, a German woman who speaks perfect French, approaches us. She is very beautiful, with an intelligent look. On her sleeve are two interlocking triangles, one yellow and one black, which form a strange six-pointed star. She comes across well and we all immediately take to her.

'Why aren't you wearing the red triangle like us?' we ask her.

The German woman smiles.

'The black triangle,' she explains, 'means prostitution. The yellow, Jew. It means that I, a German, have prostituted myself with a Jew. The truth of the matter is that I am Aryan,' – she emphasises the word ironically – 'and I married a Jew. When the Nazis came to power, they gave me an ultimatum: divorce or go to prison. I refused to divorce. And here I am.'

There is a quiet strength in her words, an extraordinary dignity. Women like her allow you to believe in the future of a new Germany.

HASAG *KOMMANDO* (LEIPZIG, GERMANY)

The journey is short. We go in the familiar cattle wagons, with the inevitable communal bucket and the resulting stench. But, by next morning, we have already reached the end of our journey, that is, the concentration camp built next to Leipzig, a short distance from the HASAG iron and steel works where we are destined to work.[25]

Much has been said about the Gestapo henchmen, the SS monsters, but we mustn't forget they were nothing more than evil executioners. However, the leading role played by the great magnates of German industry, who unscrupulously exploited the deportees, forcing them, in the middle of the twentieth century, to work as in times of slavery, has been left somewhat in the shadows. Barely fed, working exhausting hours at the hardest and most dangerous jobs, beaten, without sleep, subjected to hour after hour of roll call every day, and with the *Zyklon* gas hanging over their heads like the sword of Damocles. What if an accident, an illness renders them useless? To the gas chamber! Other deportees will arrive to replace them. Labour was cheap. Their cold statistics gave each deportee an average lifespan of nine months.

There are 6,000 of us women who come to HASAG to take part in the war industry of the Greater Reich. We come from every nationality of Europe. There are female factory workers and professionals, shopkeepers, doctors, peasants, Red Army officers, women of modest means and others from the more affluent classes. Nevertheless, despite the differences in nationality, social background and religious and political beliefs, we'll fight together against Nazism.

The camp, like Ravensbrück, is surrounded by electric fences and watchtowers. As soon as we get off the train, without letting us go to the block, it's time for the roll call.

I can't imagine where they found the female SS officers of the *kommando*. My God, they are hideous! They must have been hand-picked. When we are all in impeccable formation, a dreadful wolfhound makes his triumphal entrance, bringing behind him, holding the leash, the SS camp commandant. The commandant is tall, blond, all arms and legs. He walks gracelessly and has the snout of a rat, a blue-eyed rat. Evidently the Nordic race, 'the jewel of the earth' (*Günther dixit*), also has defects that engender hideous monsters.

He takes a few steps and says something that the prisoner with him translates into Polish and a pidgin French: all the prisoners fluent in German are invited to make themselves known.

Hanka, a very pleasant young Polish woman who speaks perfect German and French is among those who step forward. Using her as an interpreter, the commandant informs us that the following detainees will go out to work that afternoon:

'...4,067, 4,068...'

'Damn it, to work!' grumbles Constanza. 'They don't waste any time.'

Once the *appell* is over, we finally go to the blocks. There is a straw mattress for each of us, rather than one between two as it was in Ravensbrück. The mattress is made of rough sackcloth filled with straw. A dark blanket for each of us, like the military ones. The beds are arranged on four stacked levels. There is a *waschraum* with lots of taps, where we can properly wash ourselves, though without soap of course.[26]

At noon, they hand out a fairly thick soup, edible and abundant. That first day, our impressions are not too bad. We think the *kommando* is better than the life we knew in Saarbrücken and Ravensbrück.

After lunch, chop chop, *schnell!*, and off we go to our designated work. We make a short journey, watched by a large group of SS officers, armed and accompanied by fierce dogs. We believe we are heading towards a factory or workshop and are therefore very surprised when we see the work that awaits us. They take us to a factory that has been bombed. The task there is to try to recuperate everything from the basement canteen, the roof of which is half caved-in, and in a very precarious state. Setting foot inside means taking your life into your hands. Screaming and hitting us, they force us downstairs. Ah, but of course the brave defenders of the Greater Reich remain outside, surrounding the bombed-out factory at a safe distance.

We've been given instructions to recover and bring out a large quantity of cardboard boxes full of crystal glasses left in the basement. To get there, we have to cross a veritable obstacle course. We organise a chain, working slowly, reluctantly. We are all different nationalities. We can't understand each other: we look at one another. Can we trust each other?

Suddenly, someone trips and drops a box, with a loud crash of breaking glass. Everyone bursts out laughing. It's like a signal. We break all the glasses, ruthlessly. We don't leave a single one intact.

Once the *crystalicide* is over, we emerge from the basement euphoric, smiling at each other, terribly proud of our first sabotage. 'It has to start somewhere', as they say.

Before going back to the camp, we're lined up and searched by the SS. Some who have picked up bits and pieces from the collapsed basement are given a few slaps. And then it's *raus schnell!*, back to the camp.

The following afternoon, when I return – alone, without Constanza – to the bombed-out factory, I notice a building with working machines near where I have been sent to collect bricks. The wall is half destroyed, allowing me to see inside.

A blond lad stares out at me and makes a small gesture of sympathy.

'Political prisoner?' I ask him.

The lad turns his back, answering my question. Painted on the back of his jacket are the letters KG (*kriegs gefangen*, prisoner of war).

'And you?' he asks with his eyes, making a gesture with his chin. 'Political.'

He smiles. I want to know something else.

'*Français?*'

He shakes his head.

'*English, Polski, Ruski?*'

The blond lad keeps shaking his head. In the end, he writes an N with his index finger. Netherlands.

Another lad, probably a compatriot, approaches him. He also has the letters KG printed on his jacket. He smiles at me, and they whisper among themselves. Then, looking left and right, they throw a tiny package wrapped in newspaper that lands right at my feet. Cigarettes.

Fortunately, I'm not searched, and I arrive back at the camp with my booty. A French woman who speaks German takes the paper and translates it for us: it's a war communique. With insane joy, we learn that Hitler's forces are, as Constanza would say, 'getting a real thrashing'. What a joyous day!

They never did make us go back to the bombed-out factory.

One morning, lined up in perfect rows before the commandant, with Hanka beside him, roll call begins.

What's happening? The *blockovas*, nervous, are screaming hysterically. The SS officers count and recount. The commandant is growing visibly impatient.

In the end it dawns on us: there's someone missing. Two female SS go back to the huts and return a little later dragging a young Soviet woman, a girl who had stayed sleeping on her pallet.

The two SS guards viciously lash out at the poor woman. They punch her in the face, arms, wherever they can. Huge purple marks begin to bloom on her face and neck.

A Frenchwoman in the front row can't contain herself and lets out an outraged 'Oh!'. Suddenly, leaving the Soviet woman, the SS officers launch themselves like wild beasts at the one who dared protest. Brutally dragging her out, right there in front of us in our rows, they start whipping her mercilessly. The commandant raises his gloved hand. Is he going to stop the savagery? He coldly turns to Hanka and says something to her. We see the colour drain from her face and she makes a movement, as if hesitating. Eventually, she goes off. A few seconds later she reappears, hanging her head, not daring to look at us. In her hands she is holding the commandant's whip. He simply wanted to join in the 'party'. Taking his time, he gives the order to haul the Frenchwoman down the basement stairs. The two SS officers grab her, facedown, dragging her by the legs. The poor wretch's face smashes against the concrete steps.

'*On vous aura!*' (We will defeat you!), the tormented woman screams at them bravely.

Once downstairs, the three whip her until they've had their fill. That night, our comrade sleeps in the 'bunker', that is, the dungeon.[27]

When we see her the next morning, we're horrified. Her whole body is bruised. And the poor Soviet girl's cheeks, forehead, eyelids and neck are monstrously swollen and bruised. She will never recover from the trauma.

That day there is another victim: Hanka. Our young girl, our dear Hanka, becomes yet another *kapo*, obediently fetching the commandant's whip, smiling at him, feeding his dog. The reward for her services a bowl of good soup from the SS kitchen.

There are eight Spanish women in the *kommando*.

Our doyenne, Conxita, is a *baturrica* (that is, from Aragon), a woman in her forties, who always has a smile on her face and with unending good humour. She and her husband have provided false documentation to the Resistance. Having arrived in France at a young age, they speak a colourful mixture of Spanish and French.

'*Arrivaron los alemanes, arretaron a mi marí, volaron las pulas y tuaron el chien. Qué malor!* (The Germans arrived, arrested my husband, stole the chickens and killed the dog. Disgraceful!)'

Our Conxita sings *jotas* like an angel, in a mixture of Castilian Spanish and Aragonese. She's like a mother to all of us.

Carmeta, a textile worker from Barcelona, has the common sense and ability to go straight to the root of the most difficult problems, typical of true proletarians. Tiny, ever-cheerful, diligent, very good at doing lots of things, she's like a little mouse, always on the move. She collects everything: papers, dirty rags from the factory, shoelaces. She cleans the rags and uses them to make handkerchiefs, bras, little bags, whatever she can. Carmeta has an unfailing morale; she never complains, never loses her head, is very sincere and very fair; she's forthright when she criticises you but doesn't lose her temper if you criticise her. Carmeta is a communist.

Elisa is as bold as María. Unrivalled in the art of thinking on her feet, she's always able to improvise a plan. A convinced anarchist, staunch supporter of 'free love', when she speaks of thieves, she modestly calls them 'those who live by attacking capital', which makes us all roar with laughter. We have always got on very well with her. She's a solid woman, and one you can count on for anything.

Mercedes, a young married woman, has stood by her husband out of love. He is effectively an agent in the British Intelligence Service, and she naively confesses that she never imagined she would pay such a high price. In spite of everything, she faces the situation head on and knows how to behave with dignity.

Marita, from Alicante, is from a well-off family. She and her husband, an engineer, have been active in the Resistance. The hunger and discomfort really get to her, but she can take it. We tease her for the way she talks about her beloved oven-crusted rice as if she were actually tasting it. I have no idea how many women – of every nationality – in the camp, have been given Marita's fabulous recipe: 'And at the end, you beat some eggs, pour them on top and put it under a very hot oven for a moment...'

Marita isn't the only one who shares recipes. It's like an obsession. You see a woman surrounded by other hungry women, all with little pencil stubs and scraps of paper taken from who-knows-where, taking notes, their eyes feverish, salivating, their hunger more acute than ever and hear phrases that give you goosebumps: 'once the chicken is well browned, you add the champagne...'. I avoid these groups like the plague and when someone asks me, 'And how do you make Spanish rice?' I cut them off immediately, because just remembering that delicious rice casserole my mother used to make makes me feel nauseous.

Let's leave the food and go back to the Spanish women.

Elisa and María provide the solution to a very major problem. As I have already said, we've been given a dress, shirt and knickers, as well as some very thick woollen stockings that they distributed at HASAG. But there is so much we don't have. How, for example, are we to wash the dress? At any moment, day or night, they can summon us for roll call. Showing up without our uniform earns us a good beating. Going out and standing still for hours in a wet dress, pneumonia. And pneumonia can lead to the crematorium. With their customary lack of logic, the Nazis don't give us a change of clothes, but they do insist that we are always clean and neat. And woe betide you if you're dirty! Cleanliness is inoculated via beatings and whippings.

Well, Elisa and María, Lord knows how – *comme ci comme ça* – manage to bring us a complete, brand-new change of clothes. So each of the eight of us can wash our clothes every week and put on the 'recovered' clothes while waiting for ours to dry. When it is sufficiently dirty, we wash it and that day no one can change. We do this the whole time we're there, carefully respecting the turns, without ever being found out thankfully, for it would have cost us a good thrashing.

The notion of having clean clothes to wear is no trifling matter. It represents a very important aspect of defending our human dignity. We mustn't let ourselves go.

In rows, marching in step and well-guarded by dogs and SS officials, we go to work at the HASAG factory. Constanza, María and I are assigned to the Nordwerk department to work on automatic lathes and shell cleaning.

The factory is huge, overwhelming and makes artillery shells of various sizes. In addition to the 6,000 deportees, prisoners of war and forced labourers from all over Europe, there are a very small number of conscripted German workers who generally perform the roles of supervisors or technicians. Clearly the German war industry only functioned in those days thanks to foreign and forced labour.

They line us up and the *obermeister*, that is, the foreman, makes an appearance. As if he were choosing horses at a fair, he looks us up and down, occasionally squeezing our biceps.

'All that's left for him to do is make us show our teeth, like donkeys,' María grumbles.

In the end, the boss says he needs three strong women. María and I, two sturdy oak trees in the back row, shrug and slump our shoulders.

The *obermeister* makes his choice and then carries on pacing up and down.

'I need two very intelligent women.'

I almost laugh when I notice the imbecilic expression that María immediately adopts, which I then imitate. Suddenly, the *obermeister* stops pacing at the front, moves to the back rows and slaps María and I on the shoulder.

'*Sie und sie*'. (You and you).

Fuming, we go to the machines. The job consists of passing a shell through a gauge. If it just fits through, the shell is good. If it doesn't go through, it has to be sent for deburring. And if it wobbles, it has to be scrapped. To do this they need 'very intelligent women'. It's just like it was in the army: who knows how to play piano? Come on then, peel these potatoes!

I very conscientiously fill my time sending good shells to scrap, identifying defective ones as perfect and sending those with correct measurements to be deburred. Disrupting the war industry is a significant victory.

Two days later, they send me to an automatic lathe. My machine, a huge machine, is the first in a chain of four, each of which performs a different operation on the shell. In my corner, there are three parallel production lines of four machines each; and the three lines have one supervisor – a young German worker with very blond curly hair.

The worker gestures with his hands to show me what I have to do, which isn't very complicated, but I make him explain it to me repeatedly. All the while I am thinking not about how to properly carry out the task the man is describing with considerable patience, but rather of the possibilities for sabotage I have before me. How can I render the shells useless?

From time to time, I catch the blond man watching me intently. Can he read my mind? I feign indifference and work exasperatingly slowly.

In the end, the supervisor comes over and sits on a box. He points to my red triangle with no letter on it and asks me my nationality.

'Spanish.'

The man looks at me, startled.

'*Spanisches? Franco oder Pasionaria?*'[28]

'Pasionaria.'

And regarding the other name, I add a rather ugly word. The advantage of using languages you barely know is that you can brazenly drop in strong expressions that are not particularly refined.

My insolent reply brings an unmistakeable gleam of sympathy to his blue eyes. He smiles.

'Arrested for?'

'Politics.'

'Communist?'

'Yes.'

The man smiles again, and it seems to me there is a kind of complicity in his smile.

That night I lie there thinking. Each time we put a shell in the machine, you have to pull down hard on a huge lever which activates the mechanism that keeps the shells held firmly, while an automatic file rounds off the hole at the bottom of the shell. If I don't pull the lever down properly, the shell wobbles inside the machine, and the file, instead of making a round hole, goes all over the place…

The following day, anxious to put my plan into practice, I intentionally pull the lever down lightly. The shell oscillates, not held properly. The file begins to work and, overjoyed, I see that the hole in the bottom of the shell, instead of being perfectly round, takes on more of an egg-shape.

For a moment, I notice the blond German's gaze fixed on me. He looks at me with such a curious expression I am terrified.

'He's seen me. He's realised,' I say to myself. 'There's no way he hasn't noticed.'

But the man says nothing and goes to monitor another production line.

The shells are getting increasingly catastrophic and I'm ecstatic, when suddenly there is an extraordinary crack, a shell whistles out and the entire machine shakes with noise as if it were the end of the world: the shaft has broken.

I'll admit it: I freeze. I hadn't meant to go so far. Sabotage of this kind can mean hanging or a trip to the gas chambers.

The *obermeister* rushes over. He barks in such a way that I can see all his gold teeth and even down his throat.

'Sabotage! Sabotage!' he bellows, bringing his fists up to my face.

Help arrives unexpectedly in the form of the blond supervisor. Calmly, pronouncing his words clearly – undoubtedly so I can understand – the man gives his explanation. No, it isn't sabotage. 'This woman doesn't understand a word of German, nothing, absolutely nothing, *nichts...*'

He's lying through his teeth. Hugely emotional, I see that the worker has observed my sabotage and not only turned a blind eye but facilitated it and is now making excuses to save my life.

The *obermeister* stops bellowing, calls a Russian *kapo* and makes her translate. I give a meaningful shrug. He then calls a French woman to interpret, an admirable woman we call Marie Lorraine, because she originates from that region. Marie Lorraine, impassive, 'translates' what the *obermeister* says, or rather she begins by saying to me loudly in front of him, 'This cuckold wants me to say...' and ending with, 'but you don't understand, you don't speak French.' Wonderful Marie Lorraine!

Naturally, I shrug my shoulders again: 'I don't understand' French. Desperately, the *obermeister* shakes my arm, pointing to my red triangle devoid of letters.

'What nationality?' he repeats, bellowing like a wild beast. 'French, Czech, Polish?'

'*Spanisches!*' I eventually say, with a pride that isn't feigned.

'Ah!' grumbles the *obermeister* in a quieter tone, almost with a certain respect.

He then gives an order to the blond man. He's to take me to the work in the shell bath, the acid. It's a severe punishment, because the foul acids soon kill off the unfortunate prisoners who work there. Despite everything, I'm happy, because the greatest danger has passed. But even happier for having found a comrade in Hitler's Germany. I could have smothered him with kisses.

The blond, leaving me at my workstation, flashes me a knowing smile.

'*Morgen*, tomorrow I will come and look for you.'

He keeps his word. The following day, he gestures to me and leads me to a huge machine, with another automatic lathe. Maybe he wants me wreck this one too. Just to be on the safe side, I behave myself for a few days, though not too many.

Because of my accidental feat, they have to remove the broken machine with cranes and chains, meaning all four machines in the production line come to a standstill for ten days. Given that seven hundred shells come off the line every day, this constitutes a loss of 7,000 shells for the Greater Reich.

After the initial fear has passed, I strut around boastfully, forgetting that my 'heroism' was actually quite unintentional.

Life is hard for us. For a week we start work at five in the morning and finish at five in the afternoon. Before leaving, we have to endure the inevitable roll call, never less than an hour long. And when we return, another hour, never less, of roll call. At noon, they take us to the camp to eat. We have to wolf down the soup quickly and then, come on! line up, and back to work.

The following week we work from five in the afternoon to five in the morning, which doesn't mean they let us off roll call. We always work on our feet, doing tough jobs; exhausting and many of them extremely dangerous.

We have soup at noon, which in the beginning is thick and fairly decent, but which gets worse and worse and ends up being made from beetroot or potato peelings. That's it. That's all there is on the daily menu. For supper we are given our daily bread ration – a dark slice, sometimes mouldy and a smear of margarine as thick as your little finger. In the morning, a dark sugary water with an unpleasant aftertaste is what serves as coffee. As a bonus, on the occasional Sunday, not on every one, we get a spoonful of something pretending to be jam. And nothing more.

At first, they would give us three boiled potatoes with their skin on, twice a week. This was in the early days, but clearly they must think it too expensive, as they stop giving us them. The food is getting worse every day, and the portions smaller. It's a miracle we survive on what they give us.

With empty stomachs, working barbarically, standing for hours and hours of *appell* every day, immobile in the snow, rain or cold, barely sleeping, illnesses and accidents abound. Especially at the end of the week, at night, when terrible accidents occur as a result of extreme exhaustion. A Jewish girl loses her arm, a French woman has her hand crushed. Only the survival instinct keeps us going. And the survival instinct is certainly strong! You see women working away who are living corpses, physically broken, for they know that if they stop the dreaded 'transport' awaits them.[29] Nobody goes to the infirmary except when there's no choice, because we know that a stay in the *revier*,[30] where sinister Nazi doctors roam like vultures, is the surest way to be selected for the 'transport', that one-way trip that ends at the crematorium, stopping at the gas chamber along the way.

The awful reality is that all of us, sooner or later, are destined for the crematorium. We might last a few months, a year at most, not much longer. The Nazi 'theorists' have calculated nine months. It's all perfectly planned and if, according to the industrial magnates, they keep us alive, it is only because they need pawns to keep the Greater Reich war machine going.

Our only hope of survival is the fascist armies being crushed. 'Will victory come in time for me?' every prisoner asks, helplessly watching the rapid degradation of her own body.

A French prisoner, young Nanou, is expecting a baby. She's managed to hide her condition, but her health is quickly deteriorating. Between us, we try to give her extra food. This is possible at the start, when we are still given potatoes twice a week. The French communists – about fifty of them – decide to each give the future mother a potato every week. Constanza, Carmeta and I decide to do the same.

They give you three potatoes. One is small and pitted. No one would have blamed you for giving that one. You were so hungry! But pitying the girl, everyone ends up giving the biggest, the best; everyone triumphs in the hard battle with themselves, everyone makes sure solidarity – beautiful, strong, magnificent solidarity – wins out.

Each week, without fail, we honourably hand over the potatoes that might just be the salvation of the young mother and her child. Will liberation come in time?

No, it didn't come soon enough. One dreadful day, Nanou's condition was discovered as she was beginning to show, and the poor girl was taken to the fateful 'transport'. We can all imagine the tragic end she met.

One day, the women from another section of HASAG arrive at the camp in a flurry of excitement.

'A machine has exploded,' they tell us, 'and two Germans were killed.'

The news spreads through the camp like wildfire.

Elisa, pale, approaches us.

'It was me.'

Our excitement is at fever pitch.

'You? How did you do it?'

'I emptied the explosives from the shells that were rejected, but recoverable. Then I had to pass them through a machine to deburr them...'

Elisa had left a small amount of explosive in each of the shells and inserted them. The explosive accumulated inside the machine, causing it to explode. It was a miracle Elisa herself wasn't blown to bits. The prospect probably wouldn't have made her waver for a second. She's a brave woman.

Since we're talking about risky undertakings, I have to say María is no slouch either. A mechanic by profession, she collects the scraps of steel, which, using her own machine, she skilfully makes into knives, real combat weapons. 'Just in case' she says resolutely. And coming from María this isn't bravado.

Our machines have a meter. An average of seven hundred shells a day are required of us. On several occasions, María has been punished with *strafarbeit* – overtime – for not having reached the required target. One day she gets angry and decides to cheat the meter. She then 'reaches' her seven hundred shells a day and even allows herself the luxury of exceeding them.

This continues for a while. Unfortunately, a Polish man – probably a volunteer – who works the machine next to her and fails to meet the quota reports María to the *obermeister*. He catches her *in fraganti*. It's a serious matter and could lead to a 'transport' or an almighty beating.

Solidarity reaches new heights. Several German supervisors speak to the *obermeister*.

'We're professionals,' they say, 'and we consider ourselves incapable of meeting a daily quota of seven hundred shells. Much less a girl with no experience. But despite that, you've carried on demanding it and punished her repeatedly with *strafarbeit*. The girl only wanted to avoid punishment; it wasn't sabotage.'

It seems the opinion of the German workers matters a great deal to the Nazis. They must be running out of specialists. So María's only punishment is to sleep in the bunker and spend a few days on half rations, but she still has to work every day in the factory.

We are left without knives. They are keeping too close an eye on María. What a shame!

Sometime later a group of around a hundred Jewish women arrives at the camp. With them are about thirty children, from eight to fourteen years old. After a long and painful journey, they are starving, exhausted, dirty, lice-infested. It pains us all to see them.

The women, and the children too, are immediately taken to work in the factory. The children are assigned to work with the acids. It's criminal and turns our stomachs. It's clear that this is about exterminating them quickly. But first, the war industry moguls want to exhaust their small, miserable workforce.

Solidarity surfaces once again: all the French and Spanish women decide to hand over the spoonful of jam we are occasionally given on a Sunday. Nobody refuses to do so. Giving a spoonful of jam might not seem like much, but to us it represents a real sacrifice.

Solidarity only extends their lives by a few days. Exhausted, sick, unable to bear the inhumane labour, the barbaric work rate and the roll calls imposed on them, poisoned by acid, weakened by hunger, the children's strength dwindles. The factory foremen decide to stop them working and replace them with prisoners. This means they are sentenced to death. The HASAG bosses are aware of this, but they don't lose any sleep over it. They're just children from 'inferior races'; and will be replaced by new victims. Labour is plentiful and cheap.

One day all the children, together with some of the women, the weakest ones, leave in a 'transport' towards the *Zyklon* gas. We are all devastated.

Constanza, María and I have ended up in block 9, occupied almost exclusively by Belgians. There are also a few Soviet women, not many, and a group of Yugoslavs, wonderful women, 'partisans' who have fought in the guerrillas.

The *blockova* of block 9 is Belgian – Constanza nicknames her *Manolo el Chingao*. She has a masculine appearance, short, slicked-back hair à la Valentino. I have to say she is very open and doesn't try in the least to hide her homosexual tendencies. The *stubova* Simona is 'her wife'. The two kiss and grope each other a great deal in front of us. They have a 'child': a very fat white cat called Pilou.

When they hand out the food, they line us up, and scoop the solid chunks from the bottom with a large ladle, filling first El Chingao's plate, then that of her 'wife' and finally the child, Pilou. Devoid of what little nourishment the soup had contained, they then share out what is left – pure water – to the prisoners in the barrack.

While we're dying of hunger, the fat cat Pilou takes on truly obscene proportions, and we begin to hate him with every bone in our bodies. It's not surprising that every time he walks past us, he receives a kick that sends him running off, yowling. 'When the tables are turned,' – María used to say – 'I'm going to cook that Pilou with rice...'

We have to tread carefully with El Chingao. Without actually raising her fists, one girl who stood up to her unexpectedly found herself part of a 'transport'. El Chingao, as you might imagine, got on like a house on fire with the hideous SS. Certain smiles and looks lead us to suspect that those relations reach a degree of intimacy that goes beyond simple administrative contact.

Our observations over the first months working at HASAG have led us to interesting conclusions. In the factory, despite the presence of SS officials, they refrain from mistreating us. Quite simply, whenever a prisoner commits what they believe amounts to an offence, the SS on duty, instructed by the *obermeister*, notes down the identification number of the person concerned. Later, upon arriving at the camp, during roll call they call the 'guilty' one forward and then comes the beating, the whipping or the internment in the bunker.

When the author of an offence is unknown, the reprisals are collective. Once, for example, we withstood several hours of strict roll call against a freezing wind, because one woman, unable to hold it any longer, had urinated in the corridor that led to the factory offices. A doubly undeserved punishment if you take into account the fact that we're only allowed to go to the toilet during the quarter of an hour break they allow us, and that a few thousand women have to traipse through three or four rooms in that quarter of an hour, which means if you're not lucky enough to get in you have to wait another six hours.

The fact that all these punishments are applied with utmost ferocity in the camp, in contrast with the apparently neutral attitude of the SS in the factory, shows us that the opinion of the German workers matters a great deal; so we come to the conclusion that if we want to start a fight we should do it not in the camp, which would be suicide, but in the factory.

We have also learned that they have told the German workers we're common law prisoners, thieves and prostitutes, that it is a question of 're-educating us through work', and that they must be very hard on us, abstaining from any conversation whatsoever and only giving us instructions that are strictly necessary to work.

How can we convincingly prove our political status to those workers? The idea is growing in us to stage a major action.

The Nazis themselves provide us with the opportunity. With surprise and indignation, we find out they intend to pay us a hypocritical salary – in the form of a coupon – in front of the workers, as though we were working there voluntarily. A travesty, which we are not willing to bear.

We therefore decide to publicly refuse the money in the factory and openly declare our status as political prisoners.

The plan is communicated to us by a French communist comrade, who asks that all the French prisoners discuss it; if they agree to it, an action will be carried out and all nationalities in the camp will do the same. She adds: 'What do you Spaniards think? Talk it over.'

When I recall what happened between the eight Spanish women, I still admire the simplicity, the absolute serenity with which the proposal was accepted. Of course we must reject the money! It's so obvious we don't even need to talk about it. Nobody says: 'What will they do to us?' Nobody suggests the possibility of reprisals. And it's not through ignorance. We know full well we are risking our lives. We know that at the critical moment of the action, some prisoners might back down and that those who do take part will find themselves on their way to the gas chamber the next day, if they aren't first whipped and kicked to death by the *kommando* SS.

We are eight women from different regions of Spain, of different political orientation, of very diverse social backgrounds; Conxita is already in her forties, María not yet twenty-three. But everyone's stance is the same.

'The Spaniards are all in agreement,' we inform them.

'The French too,' they tell us.

Once the decision has been taken, we look forward to the moment we can put it into practice. Each of us diligently tries to learn a short phrase in German, along the lines of:

'We are political prisoners, not free workers.'

At the Nordwerk, in the HASAG section where Constanza, María and I work, the *obermeister* arrives that morning, stands behind my machine, which is the first, looks at the number inscribed on my sleeve, jots something down in a notebook and leaves a small white piece of paper, printed with German writing, on the table where I put the shells. I look at it absently, not understanding a thing. A little further on, other women are looking at similar pieces of paper.

Suddenly Chantal, a French girl who speaks German, walks past me pushing a cart full of shells.

'Chantal, what is this?'

The girl is frightened.

'M…! *C'est l'argent.*' (it's the money).

We have to reject it. Leaving a shell in the machine, I walk past the startled supervisor and head towards the *obermeister*, with the paper in my hand.

I don't remember what I said to him. But of the short phrase in German so carefully learned, not a scrap. In Catalan, or Castilian or I don't know what language, clumsily, showing him my red triangle and shouting 'political' at him, I thrust the paper into his hand. The *obermeister* is about to write down my identification number, but a group of Soviet women who have caught on, run towards him, but instead of putting their papers in his hand, they throw them at his feet. And more, and more, and still more. Some tear the paper into pieces and toss them down, others point to their red triangles, and a Polish woman who has come from Auschwitz (a camp where prisoners' identification numbers are tattooed on their forearms), not knowing how else to explain it, thrusts her tattooed arm under his nose.

It is exultant, extraordinary. I have the incredible impression of flying among the clouds, when suddenly four great blows bring me back down to earth. It is a stumpy SS man, but I feel I've been attacked by a giant. He pushes me over to the machine, where the shell is now well and truly botched. Everywhere you look, SS guards are tirelessly handing out beatings.

The shock and emotion of the German workers is clearly visible. We have just shown that we are anti-fascist fighters. We hold our heads up proudly. We have moved beyond fear. It is the most exhilarating feeling imaginable.

An old German worker approaches my machine and bends down to grease some parts. His voice breaking with emotion, he whispers to me, '*Gut, kameradin!*' (Well done, comrade!) and adds: 'Hitler is not Germany.'

I could have said so much to him! But how could I put it into words?

> *Comrades, shoulder to shoulder,*
> *Comrades, march on,*
> *To free Thaelmann...*[31]

We sang that in the war. We did.

'No,' I finally say to him. 'Thaelmann is Germany.'

In a paroxysm of emotion, the old man nods in agreement and his eyes fill with tears.

'*Rot Front!*' I say softly.

'*Rot Front.*'

That day I understand once and for all what 'proletarian internationalism' truly means.

We return to camp in rows of five, our heads held high, striding out, proud, overjoyed. We could only top it off by singing. Not a single woman lost her nerve. On every shift, in every section, the result has been the same. And we are 6,000 of every European nation! I'll tell you the honest truth: that was one of the happiest days of my life.

We await the reprisals. But, on the contrary, the commandant and the SS seem rather dejected. What's going on? Our joy overflows when someone explains to us that the German workers have complained to the *obermeister* that many of the female workers have been beaten.

The Nazis don't give up. The *obermeister* calls every worker to his office one by one. We have decided to use a new tactic: reject the coupon, but demand better food.

When it's my turn, I find him sprawled behind a desk. He notes down my identification number and pushes the paper towards me.

'*Nein!*' (No!) – and I point to my red triangle with my finger.

Then, in a rather impertinent tone, fixing his eyes boldly, I add in a very basic German that I want 'better soup'.

The *obermeister* raises his bushy eyebrows and shrugs. All of my predecessors have said the same the thing.

'Nationality?'

'*Spanisches.*'

I say it with genuine pride, staring him straight in the eye. The *obermeister* is the first to look away, muttering something. It's strange. I think that, despite everything, the *Spanisches* inspire a certain respect in them.

The story of the coupon doesn't stop there. There are several attempts to make us accept it in the factory, to no avail. *Nein, nein, nein!* we repeat like a litany. The proud *obermeister* is like a beggar, running from one machine to the next. Some of the German workers laugh at him. He doesn't inspire much affection in the factory.

Until one day they decide to try a new tactic. They announce over the loudspeakers in the camp that instead of the customary soup, they will be serving us an extraordinary meal, a delicious fish dish. Whoever wants to eat it will have to pay for it with the coupon they will be handing out at the factory. Without the coupon, we won't be given a morsel.

Hunger has reached a climax. But in the French block where we currently find ourselves – we shed no tears when we left El Chingao, her wife and the 'child' with claws – as we listen in conspiratorial silence to the loudspeakers, both the French and Spanish women come to an agreement: we will go without. The coupon has been rejected.

When we return, the camp is filled with the mouth-watering aroma of stewed fish with all the trimmings, a veritable torture for our hungry bellies. Three hours of acute torture. That smell drives us insane.

Then suddenly, the Nazis capitulate, and to our great joy they serve us a plate of that famous fish. It's delicious. And how well we earned it!

I see the little child the moment he comes into the world. He has black eyes, bright and wide-open, still-wet hair, dark like one of our Spanish children. In that sinister death camp, this little Jewish boy is like a tiny, humble flower growing amid desolate ruins.

One of us, a woman marked with a yellow star, has carried him in her belly, hiding his existence with both fear and hope. Will he arrive in the world when freedom has been won or when we are still among the beasts? He is born in the midst of beasts. And from that moment on, his brief destiny has been irredeemably traced. The boy, a poor little Jewish boy, does not belong to the 'master' race.

The little one is only three days old when the young mother, by express order of the commandant, is made to return to the factory, to her work as a slave: twelve hours of work, hours and hours more of standing roll call. The baby suckles in vain at the already empty

DESTINED FOR THE CREMATORIUM

breasts. Barbarous treatment and starvation have extinguished the fountain of life. The child is doomed to starve to death.

In vain the mother pleads with the commandant, but he doesn't budge. What can we women do? We discuss things urgently and decide to talk it over with the French prisoners of war and the German workers.

All those who are asked show surprise, compassion, sorrow, veritable indignation, everything you'd expect; but not a drop of milk or speck of flour is given us for the little boy. 'It's not possible... we don't have... we can't...'

I don't judge them. Perhaps it's true that they can't. But we, who have risked everything, can't understand how those who are free aren't able to help in any way.

How that child clings to life! Barely drinking anything, day by day, hour by hour, his eyes fill with shadows, his body becomes light, diaphanous, his cry weaker and weaker, but still he lives.

They don't even let him die in peace. One day of 'transport', snatching him from his mother, they lock him in a cattle wagon with a group of half-dead women. The train stands on the track next to the Nordwerk. When we go to work, we hear the child crying – a weak cry, like a feeble moan. Twelve hours later, when we leave the factory, the wagon is still there. Someone thinks they can still hear crying. Perhaps it's just our imagination. The following morning, the wagon is still there.

Did one of those dying women cradle him in his final moments? We will never know. When the train finally leaves four days later, we can't bring ourselves to look at it. It proves to be a cheap 'transport' for the Greater Reich. No need for *Zyklon* gas. Straight to the crematorium!

Sunday is our best day. We refuse to allow ourselves to be reduced to animals. Though we are hungry and exhausted, we try to organise a range of activities.

I remember on one of those Sundays, in the French block, we commemorated the anniversary of the execution of the Châteaubriant Martyrs (the Nazis shot twenty-seven prisoners between the ages of seventeen and fifty-eight on 22 October 1941 in retaliation for the execution of a high-ranking German officer). In a sober, simple and poignant manner, the women describe the victims' last moments, and their dignified and courageous attitude. We all listen passionately.

Today, the spot where those twenty-seven heroes were shot is always covered in flowers.

We often sing revolutionary or folk songs, though we never sink to vulgarity. Each of us uses her own language. Polish, Soviet and Hungarian women, with their extraordinary musical instinct, sing together beautifully. The French are a little weaker in this regard. The Spaniards' trump card is Constanza, with her fresh, well-pitched voice, that always receives effusive applause. Singing together, the two of us give a great rendition of the one that goes:

> *You are tall and slim*
> *Just like your mother...*

On Saint Catherine's Day it is customary in France for single dressmakers who have reached the age of twenty-five, the *catherinettes*, to make fancy hats and walk down the street in them. The parade of our *catherinettes* in the camp is a spectacle of ingenuity and good taste: dragonflies made with gauze and wire, feathered chickens fashioned from scraps of coloured rags, inside a nest lined with straw from our pallets... everything you can possibly imagine! We spend a good while enjoying that parade, worthy of the *midinettes* of the Rue de la Paix.

In those brief moments of recreation, we manage to forget the daily humiliation of roll call and take pride in seeing that we're still human beings.

One morning when I return from the factory, I'm suddenly overwhelmed by a violent fever. My throat hurts and I can barely see. As I can't stand up, I have to go to the *revier*. The little doctor, María, a prisoner and Red Army official, examines me:

'Scarlet fever.'

I'm happy to hear it. Scarlet fever means forty days without working on the damned shells.

I therefore move to the infectious diseases barracks – a straw mattress, two rows of bunk beds – where those with scarlet fever and bacterial infections are housed together.

Doctor María has good intentions, but no medicines at all. Nor any special food. Those of us with scarlet fever, our throats full of sores, are unable to swallow the disgusting food as the pain is unbearable, but there is no alternative. The only advantage we have, and a considerable one at that, is that the SS never show their faces there. The Swastika heroes are truly terrified of infectious diseases.

I get to know Nada while there – a wonderful seventeen-year-old Yugoslavian guerrilla fighter from Gorizia. Nada proudly tells me everyone in her town is with the guerrillas and that she herself has fought, rifle in hand, on more than one occasion. Nazi repression has been utterly ruthless, and she has seen them take young children, still in nappies, never to be seen again by their mothers.

I become good friends with Nada, who speaks perfect Italian. I shamelessly speak to her in an Italian mixed with Castilian, Catalan and Galician that would make Dante turn in his grave. Yet she understands me.

Through her I also meet a group of fantastic girls, enthusiastic and brave, in the camp from Gorizia. How I remember their cries of joy the day Trieste was won! Nada jumped up and down on the bed: '*Trieste! Trieste! Lo hanno preso!*' (They've taken it!)

And now, since I have to say everything, I'll explain that back in France, after a long stay in sanatoriums and hospitals, I sent a card to Nada wishing her a happy new year. The girl replied with another very affectionate card. I could see myself one day going to Gorizia, to give those wonderful girls a hug.

But then look what happened: the Tito bombshell dropped. Tito – the Cominform said – was a traitor and an imperialist lackey and we all fell for it.[32] I remembered the naïve, passionate admiration the girls from Gorizia had for their leader. I didn't write to Nada again. I never tore up her card though, and still have it today.

Later, when it was all over and Tito was once again the revolutionary he should never have stopped being, too much time had passed to write to Nada again. I was ashamed. I will never go to Gorizia. It's a real shame.

Forty days later, we leave the infectious diseases barracks. I feel awful, completely exhausted and as if that weren't enough, I have truly violent pain in the soles of my feet that leaves me almost disabled. I can barely walk. Luckily, I have Constanza by my side. With unfailing patience, she takes me by the arm and practically drags me along when I have to go somewhere. Always making jokes, she says: 'I'm no longer number 4,067, I'm your loyal guide dog,' and barks playfully. When we bump into an SS officer or *kapo* along the way, we stop to talk, to avoid them seeing me like that.

Constanza also has very serious difficulties. Her glasses have broken. Far-sighted in the extreme, she has to feel her way. She hasn't a hope of being given a new pair. On the contrary, if they become aware of her terrible handicap, she knows it could land her a place on a 'transport'. Nevertheless, brave as always, her *Madrileñan* spirit is unfailing:

'Check mine too,' she says to me when I kill the lice on my shirt each day, for I've got no chance of spotting lice, unless they're traveling by tram...'

I go and stand by the window and furiously 'murder' all the ones hiding in the seams. They are white, fat, foul and terribly dangerous too, because they are the best way of spreading exanthematic typhus.

I eventually notice that an elderly Soviet woman stands motionless in front of that window every day. She's probably a peasant woman, and her gaze remains fixed on the barren plain we can see through the window. 'What can she be looking at?'

One day I ask her.

'Kràsnàia Armia,' (Red Army) she answers with a conviction so fierce I'm taken aback. 'That's where they will come from.'

Exactly. She was right.

One afternoon during roll call, the SS officers appear extremely agitated. The nervous *kapos* push and yell hysterically. They count and recount us, over and over again. It soon becomes clear: a prisoner is missing.

It's snowing. The cold is astonishing, I don't know how many degrees below freezing. Being forced to stand as still as statues is unbearable. The roll call goes on, hour after hour, indefinitely.

The news emerges. They know which block the unknown woman belongs to. It's the block right beside ours.

SS and *kapos* search the camp, but to no avail. In the end, they have no option but to accept the evidence: the Soviet prisoner Timotxenko has escaped.

How? We never did find out. With an accomplice on the outside, presumably. Because it is absolutely impossible to escape in the prisoner's uniform, those enormous boots without laces and the old coat they gave us recently, with huge red painted crosses front and back that you can see a mile off.

Hour upon hour we wait in that horrible roll call as punishment for Timotxenko's escape. With refined cruelty, the commandant orders the women from the escapee's block to stand for an hour of roll call without their coats, in their miserable short-sleeved uniform.

The following day, the *revier* is packed. Numerous prisoners arrive with pneumonia and breathing problems.

Emotions run high following Timotxenko's escape. We're terrified for her.

If they catch her...

But they won't. Timotxenko shows us that it is possible to escape, even from that camp which we had thought watertight. Hope and escape plans come back to the fore and once again it becomes all we talk about.

Hunger has reached a desperate level, but nobody talks about it, because we're all in the same boat and it seems rather indecent to complain to another prisoner who is just as hungry as you. Everyone tries to find ways to cheat hunger and give the sensation of eating more than you actually are. Some tear the daily slice of bread into miniscule pieces that they eat slowly, at regular intervals. Others save some of their midday soup to eat at night. I get hold of an empty tin can with a little salt from a Soviet woman who works in the kitchen. I break my little piece of bread in two, hide one half very carefully under my mattress and take the other half to the factory, together with the meagre smear of margarine we receive each day. Next to my machine is a tap, used by the German supervisors to make coffee during their break. I go to the tap, fill the tin, add the salt, margarine and the half slice of bread torn into pieces, mix it all with a spoon and imagine I'm savouring a delicious, piping hot soup. Then, over the next few hours, I start to daydream, thinking about the other half of the bread which I wolf down as soon as I get back.

One day, I return from the factory to a very unpleasant surprise: my bread has disappeared. Someone has stolen it. To say I curse the petty thief is an understatement: I feel homicidal impulses. I would strangle her.

One afternoon my friend Regina sits down at the table in the block. In front of me, she takes from a little bag a small piece of raw beetroot and starts chewing it carefully.

I have a great deal of affection for Regina. She is one of the women, an eyewitness to the Châteaubriant drama, who recounted the events with such sober emotion. She has an awful lot of common sense, is balanced and a good friend. But in that instant, all of this goes out the window, and all I can see is that juicy, red piece of beetroot, taunting my hungry belly. I feel like jumping on her and snatching it, punching her if she resists. I don't recognise myself. A strange, hoarse, inarticulate sound comes out of my throat, perhaps the same sound primitive man made in the times before language when he was goaded by hunger.

Regina looks at me.

'Are you feeling unwell?' she asks kindly in her measured voice.

Alarmed, I contemplate her face and serene eyes, and trembling with emotion I am once again a political prisoner. I force myself to smile, mumble a vague explanation, run to my bed and lie face down on the mattress, dying of shame, terrified of myself and out of my mind with hunger.

I'm getting worse by the day. My clothes are hanging off me, I have no strength and my feet are becoming more and more painful. Standing during roll call is absolute torture. Luckily, I no longer have to go to the factory.

I'm overjoyed to learn from my friends that the women's continuous and increasingly effective sabotage has caused chaos in the factory, leaving the bosses tearing their hair out. News from the front is superb. The Nazis are taking a massive beating, in Germany itself.

All those of us who don't work in the factory are taken to peel potatoes and vegetables for the SS kitchen. We are thoroughly searched as we leave, and woe betide anyone who tries to pocket a miserable potato! There is a young SS man in charge of surveillance, and instead of a whip, he uses a baton to mercilessly club his victims, horribly frequently.

One day they call us over the loudspeakers. As usual, they speak in German and Polish. We think they are telling us to go to the kitchen. We all meet there, when suddenly an SS guard comes out, some kind of giant, armed with a sizeable club. Everyone runs off as fast as their legs can carry them. I can't. The SS officer catches up with me and whacks me with the club, hard, in the centre of my back.

Self-preservation kicks in and I somehow manage to stay on my feet: I know it excites them to see a prisoner fall to the ground, and they often end up beating them to death. Running and stumbling as best I can, I reach the door of the block which isn't far off.

I feel strangely weak, as if my strength has suddenly drained from me. I sense that something very serious has just taken place in my body. From that point on, my health, already fairly dismal, begins to decline with alarming speed.

It is a difficult period. The food is getting worse. Pure water, with a few odd scraps of beetroot or potato peelings swimming in it. Bread is even scarcer. For any reason whatsoever, we are forced to do hours and hours of strict roll call. Prisoners are being taken away on 'transports' at a terrible pace.

One day, the city of Leipzig is bombed heavily over the course of several hours. Planes drop leaflets inviting the German army to surrender. We manage to find some and read them with indescribable emotion.

As a punishment for that bombing, we are left without food for twenty-four hours. That day, during roll call, the commandant with the rat's snout sadistically feeds his dog an enormous plate of meat in front of 6,000 immobile women who haven't eaten a scrap for over a day.

The loudspeakers bark something in German and Polish. All of us peeling potatoes raise our heads. 'What do they want?'

'They are saying we must go to the canteen straight away.'

'Lean on me.'

It is Madame P., a fellow scarlet fever patient. She is also in the potato *kommando*.

Fortunately, she takes me by the arm, because going up stairs is torture. I can barely stand. How much must I weigh? I have no idea. It is as if my flesh has been pulled off by the fistful. Everything; my life, love, the child I had dreamt of having, everything is over. I've known for two days. I spent the whole night coughing – a strange cough, like paper tearing. I'm spitting up a viscous substance and wiping it away with a scrap of material Carmeta brought me from the factory. Sweat covers my back, my armpits. Maybe I have caught a chill from roll call? At dawn, I sleep, a deep sleep, as if I've passed out. Someone wakes me.

'Time for roll call.'

I feel weak, dizzy, my legs are shaking, I can barely get off my sleeping mat. I suddenly remember: I have to wash the 'handkerchief'. As soon as I pick it up, I know it's all over: the handkerchief is stained with blood. Haemoptysis, meaning tuberculosis. Tuberculosis, synonymous with 'transport'.

I haven't told anyone. I think about it as I struggle along, gripping Madame P.'s arm. No, liberation won't come in time for me. Too late. And I so wanted to live!

The commandant is waiting for us in the canteen. Beside him, three or four SS women and a whole gaggle of *kapos*. A bark from the commandant, several smacks are doled out left and right, and we all get into rows as if it were roll call.

'*Ruhe!*' (Silence)

The commandant clears his throat and speaks. The *lageraltester* translates into French and Polish.

'The factory has to remove fifty women from its workforce who are not fit to work. Fifty of you will leave on the "transport". Those who are too weak to keep working should volunteer.'

There is an awful silence. The 'transport'. The end of everything. Death. The women stand motionless, pale statues.

The commandant takes a few strides, fixes us with a cold stare. Nobody speaks.

'Are there no volunteers?'

Total silence. The commandant shrugs.

'*Gut!* I'll choose them myself.'

I am in the front row. A shiver runs down my spine, I am frozen, my legs tremble; and that terrible pain in my feet... 'Don't fall, don't fall' I say to myself over and over. Stand up straight. Don't look down.

The commandant moves along slowly. He looks at me. Goodbye to everything. The end. No. He goes past without stopping. Two more strides and he points at a woman. The first. The *kapos* take her out of line and put her in front of us.

The black-gloved hand is raised again. Two more women are picked out.

Three. Three more chances for me to survive. Why that disgraceful idea, why that relief every time the commandant points out a new victim? I disgust myself. How the Nazis must enjoy seeing us like this, fear in our stomachs, trembling for our miserable lives. We should have dared to shout...

Once again, taking his time, the commandant walks along the miserable rows. His black hand makes the same gesture five more times.

Eight in total. Those who die in the gas chamber empty their bowels during the long agony. That is how Madame L. is going to die. In Romainville, she was still a strong and energetic woman. In the camp, she has become a living corpse, with a pained expression and white hair.

The commandant points his finger. Madame L. Nine. Forty-one to go.

'They suffocate them with gas,' said the woman in the Plaza del Pino, by the dog cart.

To die in front of a firing squad, shouting out, exultant, before being shot is one thing. But to die slowly, writhing in horrifying agony, while an SS guard with cold eyes watches you through a little window, mocking you...

Twenty-five. Twenty-six. All the prisoners count, holding their breath.

'Mercè,' I say to myself, 'If they point at you will say a loud *Stalingrad*. You will say it, you hear me? You have to say it!'

Thirty-eight. Thirty-nine. The rows of women condemned to death grow in front of us, as our numbers diminish. Madame L. discreetly signals to us affectionately, as if saying goodbye. A brave woman.

The commandant stops in front of me. My heart races. Now! No. He takes a woman behind me, a Belgian. Have we been standing in roll call for an hour or a century? My legs are about to give way. Weakness and – why not admit it? – fear, the fear of death, a fear that fills me from head to toe. 'Stalingrad', I repeat. Don't forget it.

The commandant goes to the other end. He now points quickly: forty-four, forty-five. Suddenly I understand: he's picking out the prisoners who wear glasses. Beside me, Madame P. hasn't realised and innocently keeps her glasses on.

'Forty-eight, forty-nine. One more and that's it.'

'Your glasses,' I whisper.

The commandant walks past Madame P., who has quickly removed her glasses, and stops in front of me. I feel the need to urinate. Idiot! If I hadn't said anything, it would have been her and not me.

The man with the rat's snout takes two strides and points at another woman. Fifty.

Done. Yelling, the *kapos* line up the pitiful group of those going to the *Zyklon* gas in rows of five.

They're leading you to death, sisters. Humiliated until the very end, meekly standing in rows, you go to be exterminated. Even your death is a mockery.

Madame P. takes my arm affectionately.

'Lucky you warned me about the glasses.'

I don't dare tell her I berated myself for having done so.

Carmeta, Constanza and I have gone down to the *waschraum* to wash. Suddenly I feel something strange in my lungs and spit out a mouthful of blood, then another; and another still.

My vision blurry, I see Carmeta and Constanza, pale and frightened, saying something I can't make out. I don't know who takes me back to the block. All I remember is the trail of blood left down the stairs.

'Don't be scared,' someone says to me.

In the block they decide to send me to the *revier*. It's dangerous, but there's no other option. Doctor María comes to visit me. She calmly and frankly explains the situation to me.

'I have no medicines and I can't even give you extra food. You have to avoid another haemoptysis and you're the only one who can do that. Stay completely still, silent. No movements, not a word. We will wash you and feed you, and that's it. *Kràsnaia Armia* (the Red Army), you know, *tovarich*? They'll be here soon.'

For twelve days, I remain absolutely still and silent. It's incredibly hard, but I want to live. I don't have another bout of haemoptysis.

There are very sick patients all around me. There is Ada Kuri, the Greek, exhausted by a terrible haemoptysis. And Nadia Krisxenko, a seventeen-year-old blonde girl who is already the image of death. There is also my friend Germaine, from Aubervilliers, the *komsomolka* Nikolaienko, Leonia the Polish woman, and so many more, whose names I never knew. And the Countess too, who is utterly exhausted and terribly aged, but somehow not so ill as the others.

Let me tell you about the Countess. In Romainville, she was still a young woman. With bright blue eyes and really rather elegant, she had the good sense not to present herself as superior and was very easy to get along with. The Count had gone to London with De Gaulle and the Gestapo had taken his wife in retaliation.

Anticipating the cold we would be met with in Germany, she had equipped herself accordingly: a magnificent fur coat, pure wool trousers and ski boots of the kind that are covered in seal skin and incredibly expensive.

All of that fantastic clothing was lost in Saarbrücken and Ravensbrück. She also left her youthful appearance there. In a short time, she has aged fifteen years and we are astonished to realise the Countess is already in her forties, approaching fifty.

Like all of us, she goes hungry, she does roll call, receives the odd beating and rejects the 'salary' the Nazis offer us in her dignified way. In other words, she behaves with integrity.

In the *revier*, since I can't move a muscle but she can, the Countess is always kind enough to pass me a glass of water or fix my pillow. I give her a faint smile. In those days, such acts could fill your soul with gratitude.

Later, we're liberated together. During those days, we have a strange and meaningful discussion.

Myself and other women ask for clothes. We have nothing besides our old prison dress. The Countess thinks it's not right that we demand clothes and she challenges me sourly:

'I don't understand you. How can you ask for clothes? I want to feel proud to walk around in my old prison uniform. You've got to have dignity.'

Although I like her, I don't see why I should let her give me lessons in dignity, so I stand up to her.

'How many days do you plan to walk around in your prison clothes: one, two? And the day after you'll go to a fashion house and they'll dress you from head to toe, while we carry on in our rags. They've taken everything from us and demanding clothes isn't begging, it's our right.'

The Countess is wise. She smiles.

'You're right.'

We parted company friends and as we leave, she affectionately takes my hands.

'Will you write to me? I want to know how your health is. I'd like you to come and visit me at the chateau.'

The idea of going to the chateau and being waited on by uniformed *domestiques* who address me in the third person doesn't really appeal to me. *Madame désire?* I would be forever tripping over the rugs, which have insisted on getting in my way my whole life; but I promise, yes, I will write to her.

I kept my word, sending her a few affectionate lines.

Much later I receive a reply. The secretary writes to me and the Countess doesn't even sign it. She says that '*Madame la Comtesse*' is very busy following the *haute couture* collections and hosting all manner of high-ranking characters at the *château*, listing them for me, truly impressive. Furthermore, *Monsieur le Comte* is soon to be named governor of an African colony, where he and *Madame la Comtesse* will have a magnificent all-white palace at their disposal, filled with *une fourmilière de domestiques noirs*.

After all this rapacious talk, she lets me know that despite everything, *Madame la Comtesse* continues to fondly remember those who were with her in the camp. Many thanks.

It could have annoyed me, but it made me laugh. When I received the letter, I was washing – myself, not a *domestique*, black or white – my only outfit so that I could put it on again clean the following morning.

There was no further correspondence.

The bombings are almost daily. The factory, already in complete chaos, closes for good. The front is fast approaching; the allies from one side and the Red Army from the other. A bomb lands in the middle of the camp and kills a Soviet prisoner and a French woman, Marinette. She could have been saved, but the SS officers forbid Doctor María, a surgeon, the necessary means to operate. What do they care about the life of a prisoner?

I start being able to get up. One day, standing by the window, I see a sight that gives me a jubilant shock. A small group of soldiers are crossing the desolate plain. Their uniforms are different, some carry rifles, others nothing; three of them are leading horses on ropes and the beasts, afraid, are refusing to walk. Some have their heads wrapped in grubby bandages, others with their arm in a sling, one is leaning on an improvised stick made from a branch. They are dirty, disorientated, with fear in their eyes, their clothes ragged and filthy.

I remember those eyes crazed with fear, those men in disarray. They are not the same men, and the uniform is that of our People's Army. It is the spring of 1938, and groups of bewildered soldiers are running through the roads and highways of Catalonia.

'Where have you come from?' asks a friend, stopping the car.

'Vedado de Zuera, without stopping,' replies a young lad, as he runs along.

We are close, very close to Barcelona. For seven years, that humiliation has stuck in my throat. And now it's the others who are running.

I gesture for Doctor María to come over. With her expert eye, she carefully studies the little group and squeezes my arm playfully.

'Home soon, *tovarich*.'

The following day, a sinister Nazi doctor appears at the *revier*. He carefully studies the patients' pale faces one by one, reads the notes at the foot of the beds. Then, with his index finger, he points to those destined for 'transport': Nadia, Ada and myself, and many others.

The 'transport'. Unexpectedly, this time being assigned to the gas chamber doesn't alarm me: 'they will get here first…'

The next morning, a deafening roar makes us jump up with violent emotion: cannon fire! In the camp, all the women are hugging, overjoyed. 'They're coming!' they all shout. The booms of the cannon sound regularly, getting closer. Guided by the sound, we can tell that the artillery is surrounding the city of Leipzig.

The joy has reached fever pitch when all the loudspeakers in the camp begin to bark. We are to evacuate the camp. The prisoners must prepare to leave immediately. It's a cruel blow.

Doctor María and Doctor Irena, another Soviet woman, an old Bolshevik who participated in the October Revolution, come into the *revier*.

'The commandant has said that all the women who aren't sick must leave. If someone who is not sick wants to stay, we will register them in the *revier* as a patient. That is all the two of us can do. Each one of you has to decide.'

The Spanish women come to see me.

'Come with us. We can help you. We'll carry you if needs be.'

The offer is generous and touches me deeply. I know they would have kept to their word, but could they really do it? Clearly not. My presence is not only tantamount to suicide – those who cannot walk are shot in the back of the neck by the SS – but it would endanger the lives of my devoted companions. I refuse.

Carmeta, enormously moved, pulls a little Republican flag from a bag.

'Take this. We made it for you. Tomorrow is 14 April. If you're free, wear it.'

We embrace and I watch them leave, grieving, convinced I will never see them again in my life.

Over 5,000 women leave the camp that night. They go on foot, always in rows of five, setting a steady pace. The SS crack their whips. From the *revier* windows, we watch them march away until their silhouettes disappear into the darkness. In the *revier*, nobody sleeps that night. The roar of the cannon is getting closer.

Early in the morning, Doctor Irena arrives at the *revier* and calls for silence. Her kind face is clouded with concern.

'The SS want everyone to leave the camp, even the sick. The only ones who can stay are those who can't walk.'

She pauses and adds:

'I don't know what they'll do with those who stay behind. Nor do I know what they'll do with those who leave. Everyone should decide for themselves. Those who want to stay I will declare as unable to evacuate. And if anyone wants to leave, I'll discharge them from the *revier*. I can do no more than that.'

There is a deathly silence. We understand. We're risking our lives with a game of heads or tails.

Without hesitating for a second, I raise my hand.

'I'll stay.'

Nikolaienko, Germaine and a few others sign up too. The doctor writes down poor Nadia and Ada's names without even consulting them. They can no longer even get out of bed.

The SS women yell impatiently, hurrying along those who are leaving. I notice some of them have taken off their uniforms. An excellent sign. They are afraid.

The prisoners leave in rows, guarded by dogs and SS officers and we watch them from the window as they move away when suddenly the *revier* door opens and with indescribable joy we see Doctor María and Doctor Irena appear. Facing danger head on, ignoring the Nazis orders, they are staying with us, sharing our fate. They know – they tell us this later – that the SS are planning to mine the camp, may have already done so, and yet, despite everything, their consciences as doctors won't allow them to abandon the sick. They put their white coats back on; and – serene, clean, efficient – continue carrying out their professional duties as if it were the most natural thing in the world. Their presence is not only a powerful incentive, it is something vital. I don't know what many of us would have done without them there.

We can still make out the rows of prisoners in the distance when a woman bursts into the *revier* like a madwoman:

'*Tovarich! Tovarich!*'

Shouting, her words pouring out, she gestures, cries and laughs all at once.

When we see the extraordinary emotion and the victorious shouts of all the Soviet women, we understand something momentous is happening.

'We're free!' a woman translates with exaltation. 'Free, comrades! The SS have all left.'

Even the dying women rise from their beds. We laugh, cry, hug. I don't have the words to describe that unforgettable moment. I only remember that my first reflex was to put on that little Republican flag my Spanish sisters had made so lovingly for me.

It is 14 April 1945.

LIBERATION

For five endless days, the liberation armies don't appear at the camp. Five days in which we must improvise in order to survive, starting with raiding the pantry and the SS uniform wardrobe, fortunately well stocked. They certainly hadn't been going hungry!

Shells pass overhead constantly. We hear the sound of machine guns, shots and explosions all around us. It feels like the end of the world.

Early in the morning of 19 April, an American soldier appears, rifle in hand, helmet camouflaged with leaves, a sort of living shrub that seems to us the most handsome man on earth. At last!

The American soldiers shake our hands. Some, upon seeing our incredible physical wretchedness, break down and cry.

We believe the American army will immediately rush to take care of us. We are naïve. The fraternal contact with the soldiers is one thing and the behaviour of the commanders is quite another. A high-ranking American military medic comes into the camp, chewing gum, hurrying past the handful of exhausted women – some dying – with utter indifference, and announces that this is not his business and that the American army does not concern itself with civilians. I bring him the poor Nadia Kritxenko, who is dying, her eyes glassy. But that madman continues chewing his gum and repeating that he doesn't care. 'Not my business.' I could have punched him.

Luckily, another medic is with him, a Canadian, who upon seeing me so desperate says in French:

'Don't bother. He's a monster; I'll do what's necessary.'

He keeps his word. An ambulance arrives that very afternoon and we're taken to an empty maternity hospital in Leipzig. The following day, we bronchial patients are taken to the Krankenhaus St. Jakob, on the outskirts of Leipzig.

At Krankenhaus St. Jakob, the deportees, prisoners and forced labourers arrive in bewilderment; sick, broken men and women, many on the verge of death already. They take them away without even finding out their names, and many succumb without anyone knowing who they are or where they come from.

The Krankenhaus had previously been an asylum, with a beautiful, spacious park, bordered all around by very solid walls, where patients could walk and enjoy a sense of freedom despite being securely locked up. Then, as you know, Hitler liquidated the mentally ill. The master race wouldn't tolerate rejects. It therefore becomes a kind of hospital for sick deportees.

The staff who care for us are for the most part volunteers. The person in charge of the place, Doctor Halter, a Polish patriot, does his utmost to cure us, but there is little, very little he can do, due to the extreme exhaustion of the sick and the insufficient technical means at his disposal.

Men and women die at an appalling rate. Never in my life have I seen so many human beings die like this, on such a massive scale. It is as if they have been clinging to life until liberation, and that suddenly something had snapped. The gravediggers can't keep up.

I remember some frightful anecdotes from St. Jakob. One morning there is no water in our ward.

'There's a tap in the basement,' someone tells me.

I go down there, opening the first door I come to and stagger back, horrified: the room is filled with corpses, stacked on the piles of coal.

One afternoon two weary-looking elderly men hurry in, carrying a stretcher. On it is a deportee in a striped jacket. In the corridor, some way away, two Italian ex-prisoners and I are talking.

Straight away the *oberschwester*, the head nurse, goes over, examines the sick man and looks aghast.

'He's about to die!'

The Italians and I rush over. The man, his eyes glassy, is indeed in his final moments.

The *oberschwester* gestures helplessly, and we understand without her having to say a word. She can't give him a bed, not for just a few minutes.

The two men grumble, and their tone and gestures tell us they are in a hurry, that people are waiting for them elsewhere and that they need the stretcher.

The nurse, shrugging her shoulders, goes back to work. Every now and then she comes out, examines the dying man and utters a phrase, always the same:

'He's not dead yet.'

The two men stand beside him smoking, agitated, eyeing the clock impatiently and from time to time glancing over at the man who just won't die.

It's a dreadful scene. The two Italians and I remain beside that unknown man out of human respect, solemnly, in absolute silence. He has huge, pale eyes, blond hair that has started to go grey. Who are you, brother? I'll never know. Your loved ones will never know how, when or where you died.

The *oberschwester* comes back out. She examines the dying man's face, takes his pulse and heaves a sigh of relief.

'*Tot.* He's dead.'

The two men hastily take away the body.

Another day, walking through the park, we come across a man carrying a wheelbarrow covered with a tarpaulin. Suddenly he stumbles, the wheelbarrow tips and two naked corpses fall to the ground at my feet: a man and a woman. The man with the barrow picks them up and puts them back in, the man on top of the woman. Pointing at them, he makes a crude joke and walks off without a care in the world.

Death is all there is. Death on every corner, at every hour, day and night. We spend the day seeing death and the night dreaming of corpses.

One day, two young sisters arrive on the ward. The youngest, whose name is Margrit, is thirteen years old, the other barely fifteen. They have advanced tuberculosis. The two must have once been exceptionally pretty. They speak a language no one understands, perhaps Hungarian. We'll never know who they are or where they come from. The eldest is like a mother to the little one, despite her own suffering. She makes her eat, wipes her sweat, wraps her up, whispers fondly to her.

One night, silently, little Margrit passes away. The compassionate nurses take her away without waking her sister. But when the girl wakes in the morning and sees Margrit's empty bed, her despair knows no bounds. In vain, the same doctor, lying mercifully, tells her she's been transferred to another ward. Without eating, without sleeping, the little girl desperately screams:

'Margrit! Margrit! Margrit!...'

That devastating wail, day and night, penetrates our heart, drives us crazy. The girl screams for her little sister for two full days, until she runs out of breath.

When she died, we were all distraught.

Leonia Berkover and Ada Kuri, the Polish and Greek girls, die a few days apart. A few days before, we had been able to bring them some modest joy. The lilacs in the park had come into bloom. We cut a few branches and brought them to them. Poor little girls. You'd have thought we had given them jewels.

The young Ukrainian Nikolaienko and I often take a stroll in the park. The park must once have been magnificent. We speak as much as our limited vocabulary allows us, assisted by exaggerated hand gestures.

Nikolaienko has an obsession: when she returns to the Soviet Union, will she be able to join the Bolshevik Party? I can't understand why it worries her so much. Why would she find it hard to join the party? Before the war she was a *komsomolka* – a young communist – and the best *stakhanovite* in her village.[33] When the war began, she actively helped the partisans who were fighting in the rear. In the camp, she has a dignified attitude. She has always behaved in the very best way.

I tell her all this, but she pulls a doubtful expression: do you really think so?

Years later, I attended an international congress of resisters. The delegations were made up mainly of former deportees. In the Soviet delegation, there wasn't even one. They were all former partisans who had not allowed themselves to be taken prisoner. I was surprised and thought about what to say. Then someone explained to me, somewhat reluctantly, that all those who had allowed themselves to be captured were *a priori* people thought of as 'shady' and regarded as suspect. At this point, Nikolaienko's stubborn question took on its full meaning. She must have known.

So, if instead of hanging Zoia Kosmodemiànskaia, the Hitlerites had plunged her into the Hell of Ravensbrück, she would not have been a national heroine, but instead a 'case to be clarified'.

Let's not go on, if you don't mind. It hurts me too much.

A month later, the repatriation order arrives for Germaine and I, finally 'transported'. A car comes from the French Mission. Of all those who remained in the camp, we are the last ones to be repatriated to France.

I hug Nikolaienko tight, give the two Italian boys a wink, and Germaine and I go to say goodbye to Doctor Halter. We find him broken, in tears.

'In Hitler's time,' he tells us, 'I had to be here under the orders of a Nazi doctor, a criminal. He denied all kinds of medication to the sick deportees. "Medicines," he told me insolently, "are for the German race." Sometimes, stealing medicine or paying for them out of my own pocket, I managed to save a patient; other times I had no choice but to watch them die. At liberation, what would you have done in my place? I threw him out of here as a Nazi and a criminal and I myself took over the running of the Krankenhaus. And do you know what's happened now? The Americans have telephoned. They have reinstated the Nazi as director; I'm on the streets. And I have to hand over my patients to a Nazi criminal!'

Germaine and I, outraged, can do nothing more than express our sympathy.

THE RETURN

We have to make the journey in prehistoric wooden wagons, jumbled up with thousands of repatriated men and women volunteers returning to France after having rendered their services to the

Greater Reich. They disgust us and it turns our stomachs having them so close.

Five days, over five interminable days, we travel along Germany's ruined railway tracks, without anyone showing the slightest interest in our health or our nourishment; and yet in the guard's van next to ours, there are American soldiers with an officer, a medic and masses of food.

As we left Leipzig, they gave us a package with biscuits, chocolate, cigarettes, chewing gum and other little things. That's all.

There are lots of Germans, especially women and children on the station platforms. They wander, terrified, laden with parcels, presumably trying to get back home.

Standing by the train at one station is a sickly looking young woman, holding the hand of a little boy of around three or four years old. Beside him, an old woman holds a new-born baby. Very shabbily dressed, they look so sad and forlorn, and Germaine and I feel desperately sorry for them.

Suddenly, the volunteers on the train start rudely insulting them: '*Boches*, pigs, you're *kaputt*, aren't you?'

Frightened, the two women are on the verge of tears. The eldest boy starts to sob, clinging to his mother's skirts. The volunteers laugh and hurl more insults. As if that weren't enough, some American soldiers decide to join in and start throwing dirty papers and orange peel at the two poor women.

I see red. Sticking my head out of the window, I call the grandmother over with a wave. She sees my striped prison uniform and approaches timidly. There is silence. The volunteers and American soldiers must be asking themselves what kind of cruel trick I have in store for the old woman.

I give her a handful of biscuits; 'for the little boy' I say in a firm, loud voice. The volunteers look at me, stupefied. The American officer comes over. He is enraged.

'What are you doing? They're Germans, don't you understand that? Germans, Nazis. It's a disgrace that you...'

'Germans, yes I know,' I reply drily. 'Nazis, you don't know that. The real disgrace is that these women,' I say, pointing at the volunteers, 'who have voluntarily served Hitler, feel they can insult them. And your soldiers, instead of attacking defenceless women and children would do better to go after all the Nazis walking free in Germany.'

The volunteers all shrink away from the windows. The American, grumbling something I can't make out, goes back to his soldiers, and they all disappear too.

When the train leaves, the two women smile shyly at us. The boy desperately gobbles up the biscuits.

Crushed, exhausted, starving, we finally reach the first French village. An old man in his Sunday best who is the mayor, a small band of musicians and lots of women and children await us at the station, decorated with French flags.

A priest speaks out.

'We ask that all deportees and prisoners of war get off the train.'

Germaine and I leave, along with the thirty-two prisoners in the cattle wagon.

'Aren't there more?' asks the mayor.

'No.'

'And the others – who are they?'

'Volunteers.'

'*Les vaches!*' (*Bastards!*)

There are indignant exclamations, that descend into a cry of general disapproval:

'Out with the volunteers! Out with the traitors!'

There, on the platform of that pleasant village station, they play us the 'La Marseillaise'. Some women come over and give us baskets of eggs, greeting us in the French way, four kisses on the cheeks.

'Freshly laid by our hens today...'

The wonderful French people!

In Thionville, we go to a centre for deportees. There I am pleasantly surprised to find a large group of Spanish deportees from Mauthausen, including Quimet Olaso, Lola's husband.

We go to an office where a Jewish man, who tells us he is a Gaullist and a Resistance fighter, welcomes us warmly.

'You Spaniards,' he tells us, 'have to go separately to Nancy. There's a delegation from the Spanish government that wants to look after you.'

This seems good to us. At the allotted time, we go to the station. There is also a train with French deportees heading for Paris. I say goodbye to Germaine and those of us from Spain get ready to board the train to Nancy, when a railwayman comes over and asks if anyone among us speaks French.

Quimet and I move forward.

'Don't go to Nancy,' he says. 'What they told you about the Republican government is a lie. All that awaits you there is a concentration camp.'

We all burst out laughing. What nonsense!

But the railwayman keeps insisting. Eventually, seeing we don't believe him, he pulls out a convincing argument:

'Will you believe it if you see it written in *L'Humanité*?'

Quim and I can't stop laughing.

'Let's see it then.'

In a flash he goes to fetch the newspaper and thrusts it under our noses. It's unbelievable, but it's true. On the front page is an article, '*Qui a osé?*', signed by André Marty, from the International Brigades, denouncing the unspeakable outrage.

We soon agree on what to do. We cover up the 'S' on our triangles and decide to blend in among the deportees on the French train. If anything happens, we will ask for their solidarity. They won't refuse us.

We are still on the platform finalising the details of the operation when our Gaullist from the office suddenly comes running over, out of breath. He speaks to me.

'Whatever you do, don't go to Nancy. They've tricked you. I didn't know. I've just been told.'

An announcement blares from the loudspeakers in French:

'Spaniards, please go to the train leaving for Nancy...'

The Gaullist takes my arm, pushing me towards the French train.

'You don't understand French, so you got on the wrong train...'

We say a warm goodbye to him. An honourable man. Behind him, the railwaymen give us a friendly little farewell wave.

Once in Paris, we get off the bus that has taken us from the Gare de L'Est to the Hotel Lutetia, the meeting point for all deportees, and we are literally submerged by a multitude of anxious men and women. They are the relatives of the missing. They show us photographs, they shout out names, have you seen them? Are they alive? Sadly, we shake our heads. No, we don't know anything.

Inside the *hôtel*, tacked to the wall, are lots of photographs, names and biographical details of those missing. Have you met them? Yes, I have met two of them. The first was 'transported' after the intimate examination in Ravensbrück: she was pregnant. The other, terribly sick, was taken from HASAG in one of the final 'transports'. Not a hope.

They make us go through several offices. Cold bureaucrats pester us with questions, with no thought for the sorry state we are in. A proper police interrogation, as if we were the criminals rather than the victims.

As I am leaving an interrogation when a young deportee approaches me, looking intently at the 'S' (*Spanisches*) on my triangle. He excitedly asks me if I know a Spanish woman called Constanza.

'You are Joan, her "Scrubbing Brush", aren't you?' I reply in Catalan. Completely stunned, the boy nods. I tell him that Constanza has most likely been liberated by the Red Army, like almost all those evacuated on 13 April.

'And how did you know it was me? Did she talk about me at all?' His emotion gives away just how in love he is.

'At all? That's a good one! She talked about you day and night.'

A smile of immense happiness lights up his tanned face.

The following day Constanza arrives. The two of them come to see me in Bichat Hospital in Paris, where I spend a few days before going to Carcassonne on the hospital train. Soon after, they were married.

BACH'S TRIAL IN CARCASSONNE

When the train arrives in Carcassonne, all my comrades are waiting for me. Frightened by my appearance – 'you looked like the walking dead', they tell me later – they hug me, ask me questions, pass me around from one to another. Moved by this fraternal welcome, dizzy with weakness, but happy, I search out the familiar faces: Rafaela, López, the Toldrà couple, Amantegui, Panxita, Mascaró, 'Pablo'. Many others. Almagro isn't there.

'He died in Dachau,' López tells me.

'In the gas chamber?'

'Not even that. In the sick barracks. You know what it was like. They were left without medicine or food until they died. Every day I would get as close as I could and he, poor boy, would crawl over to the window. One day he just couldn't manage to anymore…'

'Until the very last minute,' López went on, 'comrade Almagro was heading up a very delicate mission. To carry it out he had to work in a really tough *kommando*. Time and again we told him he should leave the job as it was beyond his strength. Someone else would take over. He wouldn't accept it. He fulfilled his mission until he died of exhaustion. He is a hero, a true hero.'

López was almost in tears.

Suddenly Amantegui, our famous escapee, grabs my arm:

'Hey, chica, I have sensational news. Bach is here, in prison. He was taken prisoner when he tried to flee.'

The judge adjusts his glasses, opens a folder and takes out a large photograph.

'Do you know this individual?'

Did I know him?! Bach, his white jacket, slicked-back Valentino hair, his cold stare and that contemptuous sneer playing on his lips; Bach, as Almagro undoubtedly imagined him throughout his frightful agony; as Ballester saw him when he received the *coup de grâce*…

The pent-up emotion and hatred leave me barely able to speak.

'Yes. It's Bach.'

The judge fixes me with his intelligent gaze.

'What can you tell me about him?'

I had just suffered a pneumothorax. It's hard for me to breathe, and emotion and exhaustion make my voice tremble. Stopping regularly, on the verge of losing consciousness, I tell him everything I have to say, leaving nothing out.

The judge, who has listened to me with great attention, takes some notes and studies me with sympathetic eyes.

'What you're saying is very serious. You will have to come face-to-face with the accused. In order to do this, you will need to be taken to the prison. Are you up to it?

'Yes.'

'Do you think you'll be able to stand?'

'Yes. Don't worry.'

When I tell him, the doctor raises his arms to heaven.

'*Vous êtes folle*, you're crazy! You can't do anything of the sort!'

'Bach murdered my comrades. Whether or not you give me permission, I'll go anyway.'

The doctor makes a helpless gesture.

'These deportees! They're all the same, crazy. Well, if you insist, you'll go in an ambulance, accompanied by a nurse.'

Despite everything, there is sympathy in his voice.

I arrive at the prison in a state of extraordinary elation, trembling, feverish. The nurse tries to calm me down, giving me advice I don't even hear. Bach, Bach within reach. My murdered comrades, hunger, fear, roll call, the gas chamber, the lashings, the humiliation, all the pent-up hatred rises up, grips my throat and makes my heart pound. Oh, to spit in his face, slap him, slap him until I'm spent!

Someone helps me walk down a corridor and I enter a long room, at the end of which the judge, behind a desk, is studying some papers. Beside him, a typist.

Very attentively, the judge invites me to sit down, indicating a chair opposite the only door. Picking up the phone, he orders, 'Bring in the prisoner Bach.'

A bright line appears under the closed door. 'When a shadow interrupts this thread of light, it will be Bach arriving,' I tell myself. And just imagining it makes my heart flutter, my legs shake and I feel a kind of tingling in my hands. Staring fixedly, holding my breath, I wait. Now. Now...

Suddenly there's a metallic sound – *clink, clink, clink* – a shadow covers the line of light and the door opens.

The first thing I lay eyes on are feet shod in miserable slippers. A shackle on each ankle, a short iron chain between them. Bach enters. Not the conceited Bach, he of the white jacket and perfumed handkerchief, but a defeated man, dressed in a dark convict uniform, dirty, scruffy, unshaven, looking at me with the eyes of a cornered beast. And suddenly it's as if a bucket of cold water has been thrown over me. How could I lash out at an enemy in chains?

All the accumulated resentment overwhelms me: did he ever show compassion for anyone? I don't have an ounce of pity for him. But something stronger than all the hate ties my hands. It is, bewilderingly, the sense of my own dignity.

I leave on the verge of collapse. But I walk out with my head held high. No, Nazism has not defeated me, it has not made me employ its own methods. Because in the duel between the torturer and the tortured, it is the torturer who, inevitably and without remedy, forever loses their own dignity. If I had hit him, Bach, I would never have been able to look myself in the face again.

Bach is tried on 27 July 1945. Twenty-seven deportees: pale, other-worldly spectres, testify against him at his trial. Even the shopkeepers of Carcassonne close their doors that day. The room is packed to the rafters and hundreds of people wait in the streets to lynch the man the press have named 'the monster of the Gestapo'. He has to be escorted out of the Palace of Justice through an inconspicuous door at the rear.

Sentenced to death, Bach will be shot on 6 September 1945.

Afterwards came a lengthy parenthesis of sanatoriums, hospitals, convalescence homes, relapses and operating theatres. I have to overcome the fear of going back to normal life, re-learn, like a little girl, simple things like paying rent, going to the bakery to buy bread, saying hello to a neighbour; to get out of the moral ghetto, the 'I'm no longer like the rest of them', 'those who haven't been in the camps will never understand us'. I must never say to myself, 'I've done enough, now it's up to the young...', but rather must give myself to life completely, always walking alongside those who stride ahead, without allowing themselves, as Maragall says, 'to be led to the calm, still waters beside every port'.[34]

Biography of
Mercedes Núñez Targa

> We are the memory we have and the responsibility we accept.
> Without memory we don't exist, without responsibility perhaps
> we don't deserve to exist.
>
> José Saramago, *Lanzarote Notebooks*

Mercedes Núñez Targa was born in Barcelona on 16 January 1911
at No. 5, Calle Santa Ana, into a well-to-do family. Her mother,
Ángela Targa Guitart, was Catalan, the daughter of a chocolate maker, who had his business on the Rambla de Canaletas.
Her father, José Núñez Otero, was from the town of Bergondo in
Galicia. He moved to Barcelona and opened a jeweller's shop on
the Rambla de las Flores. He retained strong links with Galicia
and was on the board of the Centro Gallego de Barcelona (The
Galician Centre in Barcelona), where Mercedes sang in the choir
and attended lectures and talks on literature and politics.

Mercedes was given what was then considered a suitable education for young middle-class girls: piano lessons, French and
English language studies, typing and elements of accountancy.
From a young age, she was interested in the reform movements
in 1920–1930s Barcelona, soon showing her independent spirit
and desire for emancipation: 'At sixteen, against the wishes of my
family, I began to work in a film laboratory. It was like an earth-
quake for them… it was fine for poor girls to work, but not me.'
(Interview, *El Noticiero Universal*, 22 November 1980).

She continued to work with the 'Peliculas Cinematográficas
Huguet' (Huguet Cinematographic Films) in Barcelona from 1930
to 1932, also being employed as a typist at the Chilean Consulate.
She was secretary to the Chilean communist poet Pablo Neruda,
who was the consul there until he moved to Madrid in 1935.
Mercedes carried on working at the consulate until December
1936.

The proclamation of the Second Spanish Republic on 14 April 1931 and the euphoria on the streets of Barcelona was to remain with Mercedes all her life. She was the treasurer and active member of the rowing team at the women-only 'Club Femení d'Esports', founded in 1928. This led her to become one of the organisers of the 'People's Olympics', in protest at the 1936 Olympic Games taking place in Hitler's Berlin. The 'People's Olympics' came to nothing following Franco's July 1936 coup.

In 1934, she joined the 'Ateneu Enciclopèdic Popular', an educational and teaching organisation created in 1902 that was considered progressive in its programme of literary and political events. Years later, Mercedes was to confess that her father was against her involvement, condemning the Ateneu as a 'bunch of gangsters'.

Similarly, she explored the nearby Pyrenees as a member of the 'Amics del Sol'. In later life, she recalled how these excursions were vital to her when she had to cross the mountains into exile.

As her political ideas developed, she joined the Juventudes Socialistas Unificadas (JSU) (the United Socialist Youth). Subsequently, she became more committed politically as a member of the Partit Socialista Unificat de Catalunya (United Socialist Party of Catalonia). Mercedes justified her evolution from the libertarian movements in the Ateneu to the PSUC's communism due to the political context of the time:

Like all young people in Spain during the 1930s, I passionately followed the events of those years and all the political turmoil. I was a supporter of the Republic, but this never translated into concrete action. Until the very last minute, I smiled in disbelief whenever anyone mentioned the possibility that an uprising was imminent. How could the Right rebel against the Republic after the February 1936 elections, when Spain had chosen the Popular Front? It was absurd... But what I thought was absurd soon became a reality. The first gunfire in the streets of my city put paid to my peaceful existence. I could no longer remain neutral.

(p. 1)

When the Franco-led rebellion broke out on 16 July 1936, Mercedes was working in the PSUC Central Committee, situated in the 'Casa Millà' (La Pedrera, which also housed the offices of the Unión General de Trabajadores (General Workers' Union).

Unfortunately, there is no record of Mercedes' activities during the Civil War years from 1936 to 1939.

After Barcelona was evacuated by the Republicans at the end of January 1939, the Spanish Communist Party leadership gave Mercedes the task of going to Galicia to try to help reorganise the Communist Party in La Coruña. She arrived in March 1939, staying at Calle Emilia Pardo Bazán and working as a typist for commercial agent Carlos Canel from March to November 1939.

Unbeknown to her, she was being closely watched by agents from the Dirección General de Seguridad (National Security Directorate), who had come especially from Madrid, waiting for the best moment to arrest her.

She was arrested on 10 November 1939 in La Coruña. The agents searched the boarding house where she was then living in Calle Alfredo Vilas. The 'evidence' presented against her at the Consejo de Guerra (military tribunal) consisted of an inkpot with invisible ink, some blank notebooks and envelopes with compromising names and addresses written on them. She was imprisoned first in an isolation cell in the women's prison at Betanzos, then in the provincial jail in La Coruña, where she later wrote that her cell was lit by the beams from the Torre de Hércules lighthouse.

On 6 March 1940, she was taken to Ventas women's prison in Madrid, where the governor at the time was Vidal de las Pozas.

Ventas had been opened as a model prison under the Second Republic, in an attempt to make the prison system more humane. The project was led by the lawyer and parliamentarian Victoria Kent, head of the Dirección General de Prisiones (General Department of Prisons) from April 1931 to June 1932, and the prison opened in 1933. During Franco's dictatorship, it became a storehouse for women prisoners. Thousands of them were crowded there in inhuman conditions: the number of inmates grew from 500 to more than 6,000. Among them were members of the prison directorate during the Republic, most of whom were sentenced to death. When Mercedes arrived at Ventas, the inmates were still deeply affected by the execution of the 'Thirteen Roses', thirteen minors taken before a military tribunal, sentenced and shot on 5 August 1939, when the nun Carmen Castro was the prison director.

At the end of the solitary confinement wing, I step out into the extraordinary world that is Ventas prison in this Year of Our Lord 1940. A staggering number of women – pale, with hunger etched on their faces, some dressed in scraps of fabric from blankets and mattresses – are crammed into the corridors, staircases, even in the latrines. Everywhere is strewn with dozens of rolled-up sleeping mats, suitcases, earthenware jugs, cloth bags, tin plates...

(Cárcel de Ventas, 1967)

At dawn, every day, the Ventas inmates were awakened by the sound of firing squads against the walls of the nearby Cementerio del Este. They were able to count how many were shot from the number of *coups de grâce* they heard.

When Mercedes entered Ventas prison, she was still a practising Catholic, while also being a communist. In the prison, she lost her faith because of the treatment received from the nuns of the Congregación Hijas del Buen Pastor (Daughters of the Good Shepherd), of sinister reputation.

On 25 October 1940, in Las Salesas Palace of Justice, the summary military tribunal number 57634/1229 (Case No. 57634, File 4031) was held. The file consists of 4,826 pages, charging 120 people arrested following a widespread police operation throughout the north of Spain: Pamplona, Bilbao, San Sebastián, Santander, Gijón, Oviedo, and La Coruña, which dismantled the Communist Party there.

The sentences handed down the following day included ten death penalties. Among the women, two were condemned to twenty years in prison, two to sixteen years, ten to twelve years and a day; eight were acquitted. Mercedes was sentenced to twelve years and a day for 'aiding the rebellion', whereas in her opinion it was her accusers who were the rebels.

The Dirección General de Seguridad (National Security Directorate) in Madrid had a complete organigram of the Communist

Party in the north and identified Mercedes as its organiser in La Coruña.

The charges that led to the execution of ten people and the imprisonment of the women spoke of:

>...the dangerousness and political delinquency of some of the accused, their clumsy intellectual education, lacking proper ideals, moved by nothing more than the hatred and envy of the powerful, whom they believe to be privileged and upholders of an unjust social order, because they were born in proletarian backgrounds and did not know how or were unable to live adequately enough to satisfy their material needs, entertainments and vices....

In prison, Mercedes, who was a talented artist, made drawings of her companions, who sent them to their families.

Released on parole on 21 January 1942, she returned to live in her father's home in Barcelona, having to report twice monthly to the authorities. However, there was still a second charge hanging over her: that of belonging to the International Red Aid, and other Marxist organisations.

As she was leaving Ventas prison, one of her cell-mates gave her a hug and told her: 'Explain everything you've seen here... people outside need to know.' (*Cárcel de Ventas*, 1967).

Mercedes took advantage of her time in Barcelona to get in touch with people who could help her clandestine escape.

In September 1942, with the help of two Catalan friends, Pere Busquets and Carles Balagué, she crossed the Pyrenees into France, using the pseudonym Francisca Colomer, wife of Puig.

Believing she had escaped to freedom, instead she was arrested by the French police in Saillagouse, a town in French Cerdegna, in the Pyrénées-Orientales, on 7 September 1942 and sentenced to a month in Perpignan jail for 'clandestine crossing of the border' (Registre d'écrou de la Maison d'Arrêt de Perpignan, No. 2289). On 8 October 1942, she was released but immediately interned in the camp of Argelès sur Mer. By this time, this was no longer a concentration camp, but there were still traces of where so many of her compatriots had been held in dreadful conditions. Mercedes could not understand the attitude of the French Republican government towards their Spanish Republican brothers and sisters who fled into exile there in February 1939.

Back in Barcelona, there was a new arrest warrant in her name as 'an active left-wing element who has had important responsibilities in the Red cause'. This was published in the provincial *Boletín Oficial* on 14 October 1942.

In France, the situation was clear: there was nothing to be expected from Marshal Pétain's collaborationist regime, which had already recognised Franco's dictatorship. The only way for Mercedes to get out of the camp was to find a sponsor who would offer her work. The opportunity arose when someone with experience of looking after pigs was needed. Mercedes claimed to be an expert. In this way she was able to leave the camp on 23 November 1942 and go to work in the château Villerambert Julien in Caunes Minervois (in the department of Aude).

In January 1943, she began work as a cook in the headquarters of the occupying German forces in Carcassonne. By now she had made contact with local members of the French Resistance and was active in the Fifth Group of Spanish Guerrillas of the Department of Aude as a liaison, together with Rafaela Soro, with the pseudonym 'Paquita Colomer'. Later she became a sergeant in the FTPF (Francs-Tireurs et Partisans de France).

> Among the many things I had to do in France during the occupation was to send information about the regional headquarters the Germans had established in Carcassonne, where I worked as a cook.
>
> (Interview, *Faro de Vigo*, 1978)

> ...I lived legally in Carcassonne, with fake documents, and was the contact for a group of guerrillas. They were woodcutters: groups of forty, twenty of whom were legal, and while they made charcoal, the other twenty carried out the actions...
>
> (Interview, *Mundo Diario*, 16 November 1980)

> Where I lived, at, No. 20 on Rue Fabre d'Églantine, was open house for the guerrillas. It was a safe house, unknown even

to most of my comrades, which was used in exceptional
circumstances...

(Interview, *Faro de Vigo*, 1977)

In Carcassonne, she met up again with a friend from Barcelona,
the photo-journalist Agusti Centelles. Both helped produce coun-
terfeit documents for the guerrillas.

On 25 May 1944, Mercedes and eleven companions from her
guerrilla group were arrested. Among them were Gabriel Mascaró,
Pedro Torrades, Antonio Mari Font, Vicente Miralles, Pedro
Almagro, Francisco Rovira, Antonio Rodríguez, Soriano, Juan
López and Miguel Amantegui, who managed to escape in the confusion created when the train taking them to a Nazi concentration
camp was bombarded.

When Mercedes was arrested, she suffered a violent interrogation in the headquarters of the SD-Gestapo at the hands of René
Bach, a twenty-three-year-old interpreter from Alsace working
with the Gestapo, known for his participation at Haute Vallée,
when he shot and killed the guerrilla Ballester at point-blank
range, and cold-bloodedly killed other resistance fighters.

Mercedes was arrested and deported under her false name of
Francisca Colomer, wife of Puig (information supplied by International Tracing Services of the KL Buchenwald, archives of the
kommando HASAG of Leipzig-Schönefeld).

On the journey, the men were taken to the camp at Royallieu
(Frontstalag 122) at Compiègne, and the women to the Fort de
Romainville, where Mercedes met Constanza Martínez, like her a
PSUC militant.

On 14 June 1944, Mercedes and her fellow deportees were taken
by train in inhuman conditions to the Nazi concentration camps:

We were taken first to Saarbrücken, and from there to
Ravensbrück... in the five days the journey lasted, we were only
given a bit of bread and a pitcher for our bodily needs... Our
only contact with the outside world was a tiny window with
barbed wire... We were fifty-three women in a wagon for transporting horses. It was a miracle we didn't succumb.

(Interview, *El Periódico*, 21 November 1980)

Mercedes arrived at Ravensbrück on 23 June 1944.

When we reached the station at Fürstenberg, we were made to walk several kilometres to the camp. On the way we saw pretty houses with gardens where children were playing happily among the flowers. That sweet scene stirred our hearts as women. But what terrible irony! The children were the children of our guards. The flowers we were admiring owed their splendour to the fact that the soil was fertilised with the ashes from prisoners incinerated in the crematoriums. When we arrived, I thought I would pass out. The SS were waiting for us with sticks and dogs. It looked like the Apocalypse.

(Interview, *El Periódico*, 21 November 1980)

…When we reached the camp, we were put into quarantine, shut up in a barracks, so that they could start the selection process… they put us through several tests to decide those who were fit for work and those who weren't. That meant that these last ones were destined for the 'gas'… the old and the sick… were separated and liquidated…

'Look,' said one woman. 'There are the kitchens. Can't you see the smoke from the chimney?'

It was the crematorium.

(Interview with Montserrat Minobis, November 1980)

From that moment on, Mercedes was simply a number: No. 43225, one of the 140,000 women in the camp, of whom around one hundred were Spanish Republicans. She was imprisoned there for forty days, meeting companions such as Neus Catalá, Geneviève Anthonioz-De Gaulle, Lise London… On 21 July 1944, she was sent to the *kommando* HASAG, outside Leipzig, with ID number 4068. Among the 6,000 women in the *kommando* were eight Spanish women who helped and supported one another: Constanza Martínez Prieto, Carme Boatell, Mercedes Bernal, Marita, Elisa Ruiz, María Ferrer (known as Contxita), María Benitez Luque and Mercedes Núñez Targa, known as Paquita.

In the *kommando*, Mercedes, together with other women, carried out acts of sabotage to render the artillery shells they were making useless:

> Really, when we arrived at the camp, we realised it was impossible to do anything there; but when we were taken to work at the factory, we thought we could try something. And we decided that, in our desperate situation, we might as well try to sabotage the shells, as there was not much control, despite the presence of the SS and the German workers. We ruined a great quantity of shells...
>
> (Interview Montserrat Minobis, November 1980)

The women deportees were identified by a number sewn on to the striped uniforms they wore, as well as a different coloured triangle for each category of prisoner. For 'political prisoners' such as Mercedes, it was red. For Jewish women it was yellow, and blue for those deemed stateless (the colour also worn by many Spanish deportees in Mauthausen) and so on...

> Personally, and despite the fact that we were hungry and lived in constant fear of being sent to the 'gas'... what most offended me and most stayed in my memory was doubtless what they called the *appell*... For that we had to line up in rows in the camp square in all weathers, standing to attention without moving anything, your head, your hands, your feet, nothing... in perfect straight lines without moving at all... obviously this was a punishment and a count to see if anyone was missing... (as if they could)... To me this was a humiliation, yet another attempt to destroy people... they forced you to stay impassive, immobile, even if the companion next to you fell and was being beaten... and you could do absolutely nothing about it... you felt you were a coward, they had destroyed you... And that took place every day, for a couple of hours...
>
> (Interview Montserrat Minobis, November 1980)

Mercedes was liberated on 14 April 1945 by American troops from the 2nd Infantry Division, on the very day she had been put on the list for 'transport' to the gas chamber. At the time, she was in the *revier* (infirmary) at the Leipzig-Schönefeld camp with scarlet fever and tuberculosis.

> I don't know what I did the day I was liberated. I can't remember, it was such a shock. There were women who died that day, women who couldn't move and were dying in their beds, but tried to get up when they heard the news. It was madness. It was an immense joy. What I do remember is that my Spanish companions who were evacuated had made me a little Republican flag. That was on 13 April. They said to me: 'look, if you are liberated on 14 April, wear it'. I took it and did wear it. That's the only detail I remember about the day of my liberation. The rest is a bit hazy. I walked, jumped in the air, ran…
>
> (Interview, TVE-Catalunya, March 1986)

Soon afterwards, the deported women were repatriated to their home countries, except for the Spaniards, whom nobody wanted. Franco and his brother-in-law Serrano Suñer, his Foreign Minister, considered them as stateless. In the end, Mercedes and some of her companions were repatriated to France on 24 May 1945.

On 27 July 1945, while she was a patient in the Hospital Bichat in Paris, she travelled by train to Carcassonne to participate as one of the twenty-seven witnesses for the prosecution in the trial of René Bach, her Gestapo torturer. Bach was sentenced to death and shot in September of the same year.

Some months later, when Mercedes was in a convalescent home in Meillon (Basses-Pyrénées) run by the Unitarian Service Committee (an annex of the Hospital Varsovia in Toulouse), she met Medardo Iglesias Martín, a former captain in the Madrid Assault Guards, who had been interned in camps in North Africa following a lengthy voyage on the British ship the *SS Stanbrook*, which took him with 2,835 others from the port of Alicante on 28 March 1939 to Oran in Algeria.

In September 1947, Mercedes and Medardo went to live in Drancy, on the outskirts of Paris. Their house became the meeting place for many clandestine Spanish militants, ex-prisoners and intellectuals.

Only people who have known exile know what it is like... exile isn't very romantic... it's very prosaic, very tough... too tough. And it's not only being separated from one's family and one's country, which in itself is very hard, but we also found that we didn't assimilate with the culture we ended up in and at the same time, we had lost ours.

(Interview, Montserrat Minobis, November 1980)

...We spent years with our suitcases packed, expecting the return to Spain from one moment to the next...

(Interview *Faro de Vigo*, 1977)

Despite the advice of doctors, in 1949 she gave birth to her son, Pablo. She continued to suffer serious consequences from her internment and deportation, and in 1959 had one lung removed.

The French government awarded her the Légion d'Honneur (the highest civilian award in France) in 1959, as well as the Médaille Militaire (the highest military award), the Cross of the Resistance Volunteer Combatant, the Medal of Deportation and Internment for Acts of Resistance, the War Cross 1939–1945, and the Combatant's Cross.

As soon as she began to live in Paris, she resumed her militancy: first in the Peace Movement and the 'Union des Femmes Françaises', and later as a trade union adviser in the CGT union for Spanish migrants. She took part in conferences on deportation in many European countries, published many articles, and for several years ran a radio programme for Radio España Independiente. Because of Francoist repression against exiles, Mercedes used several pseudonyms: Andrea Docaño (Andrea being the name of her paternal grandmother, and 'O Caño' the birthplace of her paternal family in Bergondo, in Galicia), María Rosa Codesido (the name of one of her cousins and her neighbourhood in Bergondo) and Anita Dámaso or A.D. (the same initials as Andrea Docaño).

To keep the promise she made to her fellow prisoners in Ventas on the day of her release on parole, from the 1950s on, Mercedes began to write *Cárcel de Ventas*, eventually published in Paris in 1967 with a prologue by the poet Marcos Ana (imprisoned for twenty-three years in different Francoist jails), whom Mercedes had sponsored during his imprisonment.

In 1968, she participated in the re-establishment of the Communist Party of Galicia, together with leaders such as Santiago Álvarez, Enrique Lister and others, becoming a member of its first Central Committee.

At the end of the 1960s, she began to write her testimony on being part of the French Resistance and her deportation to Germany, titled *Destinada al crematorio*, published in Catalan in 1980 with the title *El Carretó dels gosso*.

In 1975, with the death of Franco, Mercedes and Medardo returned to Spain to continue their militancy and to prepare for the first democratic elections in June 1977.

In 1983, she was appointed the delegate in Galicia of the 'Association of Mauthausen and other Camps', based in Barcelona. Her task was to carry out a census of the more than 200 Galicians who died in the Nazi concentration camps.

When asked by a journalist what freedom meant to her, Mercedes replied: 'My freedom is a world of justice, where everybody can live, where there are no wars or injustices, where nobody goes hungry. That to me is freedom.' (TVE-Catalunya, March 1986).

Mercedes Núñez Targa died in Vigo (Galicia) on 4 August 1986.

On 7 February 2009, Vigo city council named a street in her honour in the Pardaiñas-Rocío neighbourhood (Bouzas-Coia).

Pablo Iglesias Núñez and Ana Bonet Solé

Illustrations

1. Mercedes as a little girl
(Archive of Pablo Iglesias
Núñez).

2. Mercedes Núñez family in Bergondo (La Coruña)
(Archive of Pablo Iglesias Núñez).

3. Portrait of Mercedes (Archive of Pablo Iglesias Núñez).

4. Outing with cousins on the Ramblas (Barcelona) in 1928. Mercedes is third from left (Archive of Pablo Iglesias Núñez).

5. Self-portrait of Mercedes in Las Ventas prison, 1941 (Archive of Pablo Iglesias Núñez).

6. Entrance to Las Ventas prison.

7. Mercedes' file for military tribunal hearing, 1940
(Archive of Pablo Iglesias Núñez).

8. Exterior of Las Ventas prison.

9. Prison workshop.

10. Holy Week procession in Las Ventas.

11. Prison workshop.

Juzgados Militares

JUZGADO ESPECIAL
DE DELITOS DE ESPIONAJE

REQUISITORIA

Mercedes Núñez Targa, de treinta y un años, natural de Barcelona, soltera, taquígrafa, hija de José y de Angela, comparecerá ante el excelentísimo señor General Juez especial de Delitos de Espionaje, en el Juzgado sito en esta plaza de Madrid, paseo del Prado, n.° 6, bajo derecha, en el plazo de quince días; bajo apercibimiento que, al no efectuar esta presentación, será declarada en rebeldía.

Madrid, 7 de octubre de 1942. — El General Juez especial, Jesualdo de la Iglesia. J-4999

12. Arrest warrant for Mercedes 1942 on spying charges. (Historical Archive of the Ministry of Defence, Madrid).

165

13. Ratification of prison sentence, 1940. (Penitentiary Institutions Archive, Madrid).

14. Mercedes' prison file. (Penitentiary Institutions Archive, Madrid).

Hoja disciplinaria de

edad ..... años, estado ..... delito .....

Imp. T. P. de Alcalá - Mod. 132

Día	Mes	Año	CORRECCIONES O CASTIGOS Y MÉRITOS CONTRAÍDOS
			trae este expediente ingresando en la misma en este día.
24	Marzo	1940	Es entregado a la Guardia Civil a los efectos ordenados en la nota anterior.
			Informes
			Buena conducta
			Betanzos 24 Marzo de 1940

15. Discipline record in Betanzos prison, 1940.
(Penitentiary Institutions Archive, Madrid).

Sr. Jefe de Servicios:

Permitirá la salida del Establecimiento, previa su identificación,
al interno del mismo QUE AL DORSO SE CITA
por DILIGENCIAS
MADRID 23 de octubre de 19 4

El Director,

Fórmula dactiloscópica

Cúmplase la precedente orden de la Dirección por el
de la entrada principal.

La Superiora;
María de Jesús P. Castro

Cumplimentada a las horas del día de la fecha.

El de la entrada principal.

16. Summons to appear before military tribunal, 1940.
(Penitentiary Institutions Archive, Madrid).

167

17. Brígida Jiménez (Peque) on the day of her trial (Brígida Jiménez family archive, La Peque).

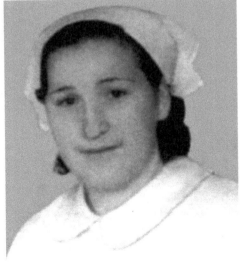

18. Nicolasa Blas Santamaría (Nicolasa Blas Santamaría family archive).

19. Map of camps in France (concentration, internment, reception, disciplinary) (FRE 39, Spanish Refugee Families of 1939, Carcassonne).

20. Argelès concentration camp.

21. Perpignan prison file of Mercedes Núñez (alias Francisca Colomer) (Archives of the Department of Pyrénées-Orientales, Perpignan).

22. Feldkommandantur, Carcassonne during the German occupation 1943–1944 (STUDIO-MARIÉ, Carcassonne).

23. German patrol in Carcassonne (STUDIO-MARIÉ, Carcassonne).

24. Headquarters of the SD-Gestapo in Carcassonne (Route de Toulouse).
Often used as a torture centre (Archive of Pablo Iglesias Núñez).

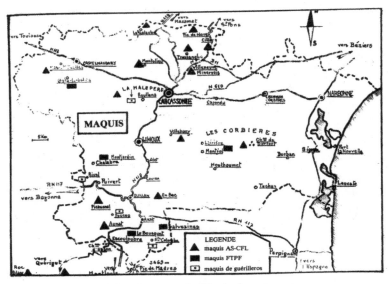

25. Maquis groups in L'Aude department.

26. Transfer of deportees in cattle trucks.

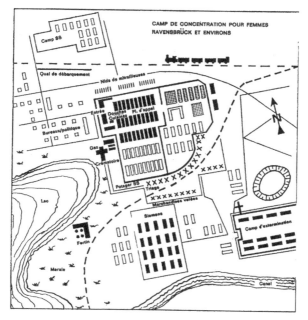

27. Map of Ravensbrück women's concentration camp (FNDIRP (National Federation of Resistance Deportees and Internees).

28. General view of the barracks (Ravensbrück Camp Memorial Archives, Germany).

173

29. Remains of the SS officers' houses in Ravensbrück
(Archive of Pablo Iglesias Núñez).

30. Himmler's visit to Ravensbrück in March 1941
(Ravensbrück Camp Memorial Archives, Germany).

31. Female SS guard (Ravensbrück Camp Memorial Archives, Germany).

32. Hangings were carried out in the rollcall square in front of the assembled prisoners. The bodies were often left hanging all day (Ravensbrück Camp Memorial Archives, Germany).

33. Ravensbrück deportees in a work kommando (Ravensbrück Camp Memorial Archives, Germany).

34. Ravensbrück deportees marked with a cross on their backs (Ravensbrück Camp Memorial Archives, Germany).

35. Crematorium ovens (Ravensbrück Camp Memorial Archives, Germany).

36. Mercedes Núñez's red triangle as a Spanish
political deportee (Archive of Pablo Iglesias Núñez).

37. Pen and ink drawings of Ravensbrück by Violette Rougier-Lecoq,
a companion of Mercedes (Drawings by Violette Rougier-Lecoq, a French
deportee to Ravensbrück).

38. Files on Mercedes Núñez (alias Francisca Colomer, wife of Puig) in the HASAG *kommando* (ITS [International Tracing Service] Archives, Bad Arolsen, Germany).

39. Hôtel Lutetia in Paris, transformed into a reception centre for deportees in May 1945.

40. Camp survivors reading notices in the Hôtel Lutetia (AFP Collection).

41. Mercedes Núñez testifying at the trial of René Bach in Carcassonne, 27 July 1945 (Archive of Pablo Iglesias Núñez).

Je sais que je vais être condamné à mort, mais je veux aussi que les autres payent.

42. René Bach during his trial (Midi Libre Archives).

43. Report on Bach's trial in the *Midi Libre* newspaper, 28 July 1945:

…Pijuan Jean, a farmer from Roullens describes the sadism of Bach during his mistreatment; Francisco Rovira, a cobbler from Carcassonne states that he clearly heard the four shots that ended Ballester's life. Rovira responded to a question by the presiding judge by stating that he heard three shots together, followed by one isolated gun report. This final shot could lead to Bach being accused of murder. Núñez, Mercedes, 34 years old from Carcassonne, was deported to Germany. Verdier, André, from Carcassonne, also deported to Germany, states that Bach was entirely responsible for his deportation…

(Midi Libre Archives)

44. Post-war diploma recognising Mercedes as a combatant in the French Resistance (Archive of Pablo Iglesias Núñez).

45. Mercedes' ID card as a member of the French Resistance (Archive of Pablo Iglesias Núñez).

46. Confirmation of rank of sergeant in French Resistance
(Archive of Pablo Iglesias Núñez).

47. *Mujeres Antifascistas Españolas* magazine, 1950, including the first
version of *Las Ventas Prison* (MCU Historical Newspaper Virtual Library:
Clandestine Press).

48. First book publication of *Las Ventas Prison*, Paris 1967.

49. Mercedes in a Toulouse sanatorium, 1947 (second on the left, top row) (Archive of Pablo Iglesias Núñez).

50. Mercedes with son Pablo and Medardo Iglesias at the border with Spain, French Basses Pyrénées, 1958 (Archive of Pablo Iglesias Núñez).

51. At a demonstration in Paris for peace in Vietnam, late 1960s (Archive of Pablo Iglesias Núñez).

52. In Barcelona at a homage to the International Brigades
(Archive of Pablo Iglesias Núñez).

53. Mercedes with her partner Medardo Iglesias at their Paris home in
the 1960s (Archive of Pablo Iglesias Núñez).

Notes

VENTAS PRISON MADRID

All of the following notes to *Ventas Prison Madrid* were added by the translators:

1. The Falange was a Fascist party established in 1934 that eventually became the main political support of the Franco regime.
2. The chotis was a popular dance in Madrid in the first half of the twentieth century.
3. 'La Madelón' was a French popular song from the First World War, revived in the late 1930s.
4. 'Facing the Sun'. The anthem of the Spanish Falange, composed by its founder José Antonio Primo de Rivera in 1935.
5. In the nineteenth century, the Carlists supported the claims of the Bourbon pretender Don Carlos to the Spanish throne. The anthem celebrates their victory at the Battle of Oriamendi in 1837. In the Spanish Civil War, they were one of the factions of Franco's Nationalists.
6. Juan Negrín, prime minister during the Second Republic, and after the Nationalist coup in 1936–1939. He died in exile in Paris.
7. The shout of Falange members, taken up by the Franco regime.
8. The convent of Las Salesas Reales in Madrid was used as the Palace of Justice in this period.
9. The JSU, or Juventudes Socialistas Unificadas, was created in April 1936 when the socialist and communist youth movements were united.
10. José Millán Astray was a general who founded the right-wing Spanish Legion and was one of the main supporters of Franco's rebellion. Best known for his slogan: 'Viva la muerte!' (Long Live Death!).
11. La Montaña was a military barracks in Madrid. Occupied by Nationalist forces in the first days after the 1936 coup, it was attacked by Republican supporters and many of its defenders massacred.
12. General Eduardo López Ochoa led the repression of the uprising in Asturias in 1934. He was awaiting trial in a military hospital in Madrid after the 1936 coup, when he was dragged out and shot. His severed head was carried round the streets.
13. Félix Lope de Vega Carpio (1562–1635) was a major poet of Spain's 'golden century'.
14. During the Civil War, many political parties and factions had irregular forces or *checas*, who seized suspects and either shot them or took them to secret detention centres to be tortured.

15. The yoke and arrows were originally the symbol of the union of Aragon and Castille in the fifteenth century, it became the emblem of the Falange when it was founded in 1934, and a major symbol of the Franco regime.

16. Juan March was a business tycoon in the 1920s and 1930s. During the Second Republic, he was jailed for tobacco smuggling and arms trafficking. He escaped prison by bribing a guard, and fled to Gibraltar. He became one of the Franco regime's most important financial backers.

17. Julio Romero de Torres (1874–1930) was a Spanish painter best known for his romantic portraits of young women.

18. The International Brigades were made up of as many as 50,000 volunteers from many countries who went to fight on the Republican side during the Spanish Civil War. The brigades were officially disbanded in 1938, when defeat became obvious.

19. The 'bienio negro' refers to the two years between 1933–1935 when political violence and increasing polarisation caused the near collapse of the Second Republic.

20. Segismundo Casado was one of the leaders of the coup against Negrín's Popular Front government in March 1939. This led to the arrest and imprisonment of many Communists, who were handed over to the triumphant Nationalists.

DESTINED FOR THE CREMATORIUM

1. Faced with the embargo imposed on the Spanish Republic due to the policy of 'non-intervention', volunteers from fifty-four countries, responding to the call from the Popular Front government enlisted in the International Brigades, arriving in Spain in October 1936: United States (Abraham Lincoln Brigade), Italy (Garibaldi Brigade), Germany (Thaelmann Brigade), Ireland, Great Britain, France (Commune de Paris Brigade)... There are some 50,000 volunteers; 5,000 of them will lose their lives during the struggle.

2. 'The Fifth Spanish Guerrilla Group in the department of Aude was the first to be organised in France,' writes Antonio Molina, its first leader, 'mother cell of the other units, from which the main leaders of the guerrilla organisation emerged.' It was made up of different battalions divided into sectors:

1st Battalion: Joucou maquis (in the Rébenty valley, 12 km southwest of Quillan).
20th Battalion: Roullens maquis (southwest of Carcassonne).
3rd Battalion: Sainte-Colombe-sur-Guette (8 km south of Axat).

The three maquis formed the skeleton of the Fifth Group. The maquis contacts were: Rafaela Soro, Mercedes Núñez (alias Paquita Colomer) and María Villacampa.

3. The Gestapo (*Geheime Staatspolizei*) was the official secret political police of Nazi Germany, organised in the 1930s under the leadership of Himmler and Heydrich. It answered to the Nazi party rather than the state and was active throughout all of occupied Europe. Within the Gestapo, Adolf Eichmann was tasked with operationally managing the transportation of prisoners to the concentration and extermination camps.

4. A town located approximately 20 kilometres from Carcassonne, in France, Bram was the site of a concentration camp from the beginning of March 1939 until the end of 1940, where 35,000 Spanish Republican refugees were held in harsh conditions.

5. The Resistance maquis was made up of men and women working undercover to fight the German occupation of France. To begin with, the maquis served as a refuge for those avoiding conscription into the STO (Service du Travail Obligatoire, 'Compulsory Work Service'), which provided forced labour for Germany. The guerrillas were organised within the FTPF (Francs-Tireurs et Partisans Français) and the FFI (Forces Françaises de l'Intérieur). The living embodiment of resistance in rural areas, the maquis led many French people to participate more actively in the combat against the Germans and against the collaborationist Vichy government. They increasingly took part in the liberation of French territory.

6. The unified armed forces of Germany (Land army: *Heer*; Air force: *Luftwaffe*; Navy: *Kriegsmarine*).

7. Translator's note: Isabella II, María Isabel Luisa de Borbón y Borbón-Dos Sicilias (1830–1904), reigned 1833–1868.

8. René Bach, a twenty-two-year-old Alsatian Gestapo interpreter in the Carcassonne *Feldkommandantur*, was well known for his cruelty. On 23 May 1944, René Bach was part of a column of a German military detachment from Limoux. They raided the Vinsous farm, owned by the Cathala family, taking away their nineteen-year-old son Auguste. His charred body was later found in the rubble of Roudié farm. The autopsy revealed that the young man was tortured and mutilated, then thrown alive into the flames.

    On the way back that same day, the Germans detained two Spanish guerrillas: Francisco Ruiz Sierra, alias 'José Ballester' and Francisco Rovira. They were interrogated and beaten by Bach. The two men refused to answer questions and when Ballester defended himself against the blows, the Germans dragged him to a ditch and shot him. René Bach approached Ballester, who was still alive, placed his revolver to the back of his head and coldly finished him off.

    Bach also took part in a sweep against the Roullens maquis. Although the raid was unsuccessful, he managed to capture the guerrilla Jean Pijuan, who was beaten but remained silent.

    After the liberation, Bach, posing as a guerrilla, was arrested in Orange, where he was recognised by a former resistance fighter from Montaña Negra.

The trial against René Bach took place at the Carcassonne Courthouse on 26, 27 and 28 July 1945; as soon as it began, the entrance stairs were flooded with people. One journalist from *Midi Libre* wrote: 'The whole of Carcassonne spent the weekend at the Court.' A string of twenty-seven witnesses, camp survivors and those tortured by Bach gave evidence over the course of two days.

Bach was sentenced to death; his subsequent appeal was rejected. He was executed by firing squad on 6 September 1945 at the Romieu shooting range on the outskirts of Carcassonne.

9. Translator's note: The chorus of 'Ein Heller und ein Batzen', a German folk song written in 1830 by composer Albert von Schlippenbach. Originally written as a drinking song, it was later adopted as a marching song in the *Wehrmacht* during the Second World War.

10. Ravensbrück (meaning 'Raven's Bridge'), is a village in Germany, 80 km north of Berlin. From 1938 to 1945, the Nazi regime set up a concentration camp specially designed for women and children. The camp was built on the shores of lake Schwedtsee, in the town of Fürstenberg/Havel, in marshy land north of Brandenburg. Incorporating Lichtenburg camp in 1939, it quickly became the country's most important women's detention centre: at least 132,000 women and children were deported there, 90,000 of whom went on to be exterminated. The camp supplied female labour to German munitions industries and salt mines, both on the site itself and across seventy factories located between the Baltic Sea and Bavaria, using prisoners from all of the European countries occupied by Germany. From April 1941, men were imprisoned in an adjacent camp.

Detainees were identified by different coloured triangles according to their category: red for political prisoners, yellow for Jewish prisoners, green for common criminals, violet for Jehovah's Witnesses, black for Romani and prostitutes, etc. A letter sewn within the triangle denoted each prisoner's nationality. Some have their heads shaved immediately upon arrival at the camp. An incomplete list drawn up by the administration lists 2,528 women sent to Ravensbrück, of whom 24.9 per cent were Polish, 19.9 per cent were German, 15.1 per cent were Jewish, 15 per cent were Russian, 7.3 per cent were French, 5.4 per cent were Romani and the remaining 12.4 per cent divided into: 83.54 per cent political prisoners, 12.35 per cent 'antisocial' prisoners, 2.02 per cent common criminals, 1.11 per cent Jehovah's Witnesses, 0.78 per cent 'race shame' prisoners and 0.2 per cent of diverse cases, in addition to around a hundred Spanish Republicans. This list is one of the few documents not destroyed.

The prison population grew from 10,000 at the end of 1942 to over 45,000 in January 1945. From April to October 1944, Romani women and children were taken there following the closure of the Auschwitz camp. Then came Polish Jews – women and children from the Budapest ghetto when it closed. Most died of malnutrition.

The Ravensbrück deportees were continually abused, beaten, forced to do hard labour and killed when no longer fit to work, if they attempted to rebel or simply for no reason. Until 1942, prisoners declared unfit for work are shot. After that, the number of executions increased: they were transferred to Auschwitz and other extermination camps. Many were executed by lethal injection in the camps' infirmaries.

Starting in the summer of 1942, medical experiments are carried out on at least eighty-six prisoners, of which seventy-four are Polish. The first experiment studied the efficacy of sulphonamides in the treatment of war wounds. The second studied the regeneration of bones, muscles and nerves, as well as exploring the possibility of bone transplants. Five prisoners died during the experiments, and six were executed. The majority of the survivors suffered lifelong consequences. Four went on to give testimony in the Doctors' Trial in 1946. In January 1945, between 120 and 140 Romani women were sterilised after being promised release if they consented to be operated on.

The bodies of dead prisoners were burned in the nearby Fürstenberg crematorium until 1943, when SS authorities built a crematorium close to the camp. In Autumn 1944, a gas chamber was added. Thousands of deportees were executed before the liberation of the camp on 30 April 1945. The last murders were committed at Fürstenberg on 25 April, when eleven detainees employed at the crematorium were executed for fear that they might give evidence.

When the Red Army arrived on 30 April 1945, only 3,500 women and 300 men remained. The SS had taken the prisoners capable of walking – over 20,000 of them – on a long death march towards northern Mecklenberg. They were intercepted after several hours by a Soviet scout unit.

11. The FTP (Francs-Tireurs et Partisans). Formed in 1942, the FTP merged three French communist paramilitary organisations (Bataillons de la Jeunesse, the Organisation Spéciale and the Main-d'œuvre immigrée – MOI), under the command of Charles Tillon. Highly structured, the FTP carried out sabotage and attacks on the occupation forces. In 1945, the ORA (Organisation de Résistance de l'Armée), the AS (Armée Secrète) and the FTP merged to form the Forces Françaises de l'Intérieur (FFI), with General Kœnig as commander in chief.

12. In October 1940, Fort Romainville was requisitioned by German military command who decided to transform it into an internment camp with watchtowers and barbed wire fences. Opponents of the Nazi occupation were interred in the camp. Many of them were shot at Mont Valérien in retaliation for the actions of the Resistance.

Along with Compiègne and Drancy, it became one of the main points of transit to the Nazi concentration camps.

From February 1944, Romainville held primarily female prisoners. The best-known convoy to leave from Romainville was the 'convoy of the 31,000s' (identification numbers beginning 31...) of January 1943. Of these 230 women only 49 survived. This convoy included, among others:

- Marie-Claude Vaillant-Couturier, arrested in February 1942, for assisting the Resistance.
- Simone Sampaix, daughter of Lucien Sampaix, secretary-general of *L'Humanité* newspaper, shot by firing squad on 15 December 1941.
- Danielle Cassanova, dental surgeon, married to Laurent Casanova. Founder of the 'Union des Jeunes Filles de France' (Union of Young French Women), founding editor of *La Voix des Femmes* (Womens' Voice).
- Hélène Solomon, daughter of physicist Paul Langevin and widow of Jacques Solomon, shot on 23 May 1942.
- Marie 'Maï' Politzer, wife of philosopher Georges Politzer, editor of *L'Université Libre* (The Free University) and *La Pensée Libre* (Free Thought), executed by firing squad at Mont Valérien on 23 May 1942.
- Charlotte Delbo, secretary to Louis Jouvet, married to Georges Dudach, shot by firing squad on 23 May 1942.

When the fort was liberated on 21 August 1944, the bodies of eleven prisoners were found behind the main building, where they had been shot. In total, during the occupation, 209 prisoners were executed by firing squad at the fort; 3,900 women and 3,100 men were interned there before being deported.

13. The Quakers had an American charitable association that aided Spanish Republican refugees, distributing clothing and provisions, as well as prostheses for the mutilated.
14. Organizzazione per la Vigilanza e la Repressione dell'Antifascismo (Organisation for Vigilance and Repression of Antifascism), the secret police of the Italian Fascist regime. Created in 1927, OVRA persecuted opponents of the regime, who were brought before special courts.
15. Colonel Fabien's real name was Pierre Georges; he took part in the liberation of Paris, 25 August 1944, leading an FFI group.
16. The SS (*Schutzstaffel*, 'Protection Squadron') began as Hitler's protection unit, known for their black uniforms, organised by Himmler in 1923. In 1929, the SS comprised 280 members, rising to 50,000 when the Nazis seized power in 1933. The SS gained power year on year, especially following the elimination of the SA (*Sturmabteilung*, private assault detachment of the Nazi party). After the 'Night of the Long Knives', 30 June 1934, and the assassination of Röhm (SA Chief of Staff) and other key members of leadership, Himmler and the SS took control of all police forces. In 1936, the SS comprised 210,000 men and the *Totenkopf* (skull and crossbones) division were principally in charge of managing the concentration camps. The SS were selected based on race (pure Aryan ancestry had to be proven) and political leaning (fierce commitment to Nazi ideology).

'*Waffen-SS*' appeared after the outbreak of the Second World War. It was made up of forty divisions and was in charge of the most criminal duties. Armoured divisions throughout France engaged in brutal persecution of the maquis.

17. The Greater Reich is a German term designating the territory over which the sovereignty of a prince, king or emperor, and later that of a state is exercised.

18. 'Night and Fog' (*Nacht und Nebel*) refers to a Nazi directive that the whereabouts of political prisoners was to disappear in 'night and fog'. These prisoners, mostly French, Belgian and Dutch, had no contact with the outside world. They did not receive any packages or correspondence and were unaware that the letters they wrote would not reach their intended recipients. Not all deportees were NN prisoners, but all NN were deportees. Not all NN prisoners were condemned to death, many were sentenced to prison terms and forced labour.

19. The *Kapos* are prisoners responsible for a *kommando*. Generally chosen from those detained under common law (green triangle). They were, with rare exceptions, faithful servants of the SS, known for their brutality.

20. *Blockova* is a Polish term for a female prisoner in charge of a block (*Blockälteste* in German). Almost always common law prisoners (green triangle).

21. The *Stubova* was a female prisoner in charge of a block.

22. *Appell* is the roll call, where prisoners were made to stand in lines for hours being counted.

23. Zyklon gas (Zyklon B) was a product manufactured by German company Degesch. Initially a pesticide made with hydrogen cyanide, during the Second World War, it was used by the Nazis in the gas chambers in extermination camps.

24. The *kommando* is a workforce or service within the camp. The exterior *kommando* was an annex dependent on a camp. It was further subdivided into different work *kommandos*. Each camp had dozens of external satellite camps.

25. The company Häckel & Schneider was founded in Leipzig in 1863; in 1899, it became 'Hugo Schneider Aktiengesellschaft', known as HASAG. Nazi Party member Paul Budin was appointed general manager of HASAG and the company began manufacturing armaments, initially in a clandestine manner. In 1934, Nazi Germany legalised rearmament and HASAG expanded considerably. Under the direction of Paul Budin, numerous SS join HASAG in positions of authority.

HASAG's most important production centre was located in Leipzig. HASAG was one of the companies that used the most forced labour. In the Nuremberg Trials of 31 July 1946, Oswald Pohl, head of the WVHA (Wirtschafts-Verwaltungshauptamt) declared that due to its size, HASAG was the third largest of the private companies that used forced labour from the camps, the first two being Hermann Göring Werke and I.G. Farbenindustrie.

In July 1944, 28,000 prisoners were forced to work for HASAG, 5,000 of whom did so in the Leipzig-HASAG (Nordwerk) external *kommando* where DCA shells were manufactured.

26. The *waschraum* was a communal room for washing with a central sink and taps.

27. The camp's prison, including dungeons and torture rooms.

28. Translator's note: Isidora Dolores Ibárruri Gómez (1895–1989), known as Pasionaria ('the passionate one'), was a Spanish Republican politician of the Spanish Civil War and a member of the Spanish Communist Party, known for her slogan *¡No Pasarán!* (They shall not pass!).

29. 'Transport' refers to the convoy, transportation of deportees to the extermination camps' gas chambers.

30. In the language of the camps, the *revier* was the infirmary. Going to the infirmary was dangerous since the SS regularly sent sick patients to the gas chambers during the much-feared 'selections'.

31. Ernst Thaelmann was a German communist politician, and leader of the Communist Party of Germany (KPD) from 1925 to 1933. He was shot on Adolf Hitler's personal orders in 1944. During the Spanish Civil War, several units of German Republican volunteers were named in his honour.

32. Translator's note: The Cominform, created in 1947, was the Communist Information Bureau, which organised all communist parties in Europe under USSR control.

33. Translator's note: A *stakhanovite* is a Soviet industrial worker awarded recognition and privileges for exceptional effort and productivity.

34. Translator's note: Joan Maragall (1860–1911) was a Catalan poet, journalist and translator and the foremost member of the *modernisme* literary movement.

Bibliography

WORKS BY MERCEDES NÚÑEZ TARGA

Cárcel de Ventas. Paris: Éditions de la Librairie du Globe, colección Ebro, 1967.

Cárcere de Ventas. Prologue by Carme Vidal. Translated by Carlos Arias and Sira Vidal. Vigo: Edicións A Nosa Terra, colección Mulleres, 2005. [*Ventas Prison*, Galician edn].

El carretó dels gossos. Una catalana a Ravensbrück. Barcelona: Edicions 62, 1980. [*Destined for the Crematorium*, Catalan edn].

El carretó dels gossos. Una catalana a Ravensbrück. Prologue by Pablo Iglesias Núñez. Edicions 62, Barcelona, 2005 (2nd edn).

Destinada al crematorio. De Argelès a Ravensbrück: las vivencias de una resistente republicana española. Prologue by Xesús Alonso Montero. Translated by Pablo Iglesias Núñez and Ana Bonet Solé. Editorial Renacimiento, Biblioteca de la Memoria, Sevilla, 2011. [Destined for the Crematorium, Castilian Spanish edn].

La presó de Ventas. Records d'una empresonada (1939–1942). Prologue by Agnès Toda i Bonet. Translated by Agnès Toda i Bonet. Cossetània Edicions, Barcelona, 2008. [*Ventas Prison*, Catalan edn].

La valeur de la mémoire. D'Argelès à Ravensbrück: le parcours d'une résistante républicaine espagnole. Prologue by Jean Ortiz. Translated by Ana Bonet Solé. Editorial Renacimiento, Sevilla, 2012. [*Ventas Prison/Destined for the Crematorium*, French edn].

Der Wert der Erinnerung, Translated by Carsten Hinz. Metropol Verlag, Berlin, 2022. [*Ventas Prison/Destined for the Crematorium*, German edn].

ARTICLES WRITTEN ANONYMOUSLY BY MERCEDES NÚÑEZ TARGA

'Dos años en las cárceles franquistas' ['Two Years in Franco's Prisons']. *Mujeres antifascistas españolas*, no. 36, April 1950.

'Las trece rosas' ['The Thirteen Roses']. *Mujeres antifascistas españolas*, no. 39, September–October 1950.

'La vida de Justo López en peligro' ['Justo López's Life in Danger']. *Libertad para España*, February 1965.

These and more articles can be found in the Historical Virtual Library of the Ministry of Education, Culture and Sport, in the Clandestine Press section: http://prensahistorica.mcu.es.

Agudo, Sixto 'Blanco', *Los españoles en la Resistencia francesa y su aportación a la lucha antifranquista*. Zaragoza: Una Luna Ediciones, 2003 (pp. 56, 116 and 117).

Agudo, Sixto 'Blanco'. *En la «Resistencia» francesa*. Zaragoza: Anúbar, 1985 (p. 104).

Aixalá, Emma. *Els EZ de Catalunya. Qui sont i qué han fet*. Barcelona: Edicions La Campana, 1997 (pp. 196–197).

Alba Burgos, Graciela, and Lois Pérez Leira. 'Galegas na diáspora'. *Agers* (2006) (pp. 85–86).

Allaux, Julien. *La 2ème guerre mondiale dans l'Aude*. Épinal: Éditions du Sapin d'Or, 1986.

Alonso Montero, Xesús. *Castelao na Unión Soviética en 1938*. Vigo: Edicións Xerais, 2012 (p. 7).

Alonso Montero, Xesús. *Intelectuais marxistas e militantes comunistas en Galicia (1920–2006)*. Vigo: Edicións Xerais, 2007 (pp. 253–255).

Alonso Montero, Xesús. *Os escritores galegos ante a Guerra Civil Española*. Vigo: Editorial Galaxia, 2006 (p. 344).

Álvarez Fernández, José Ignacio. *Memoria y trauma en los testimonios de la represión franquista*. Barcelona: Anthropos Editorial, 2007 (pp. 15–16).

Amicale de Ravensbrück. *Les Françaises à Ravensbrück*. Paris: Éditions Gallimard, 1965.

Amicale des Anciens Guérilleros (Ffi). *Guérilleros en terre de France, les républicains espagnols dans la Résistance française*. Pantin: Le Temps des Cerises Éditeurs, reed. 2004, (pp. 153 and 156).

Ángel, Miguel. *Los guerrilleros españoles en Francia*. Havana: Editorial de Ciencias Sociales, 1971 (pp. 138–141).

Anthonioz de Gaulle, Geneviève. *La traversée de la nuit*. Paris: Éditions du Seuil, 1998.

Armengou, Montse, and Ricard Belis. *El convoy de los 927*. Barcelona: Plaza y Janés, 2005 (p. 186).

Armengou, Montse, and Ricard, Belis. *Ravensbrück, el infierno de las mujeres*. Barcelona: Belacqva de Ediciones, 2008 (pp. 88–122).

Audoul, France. *Ravensbrück, 150.000 femmes en enfer, 32 croquis et protraits fait au camp 1944–1945*. Paris: Ed. Le Déporté, 1966.

Aziz, Philippe. *Les camps de l'apocalypse, l'enfer de Ravensbrück*. Geneva: Ed. Vernoy, 1981.

Bengoechea, Soleda. *Las dones del PSUC, Els arbres de Farenheit*. Barcelona: Biblioteca de ciènces socials d'espai Marx, 2013 (pp. 80–81).

Beimler, Hans. *En el campo de asesinos de Dachau: cuatro semanas en poder de los bandidos pardos*. Barcelona: Ed. Europa-América, 1935.

Bernadac, Christian. *Déportation 1939/1945*. Paris: Éditions France-Empire, 1993.

Bernadac, Christian. *La libération des camps, le dernier jour de notre vie*. Paris: Éditions Michel Lafon, 1995.

Botey Alonso, Dolores. *Mis memorias. Diez años, tres meses y 120 horas de prisión.* Palma de Mallorca: Ediciones Cort, 2010.

Bouteille-Garagnon, Marie-Jeanne. *Infernal Rébus.* Moulins: Crépin-Leblond, 1946.

Cal, Antía. *Este camiño que fixemos xuntos.* Vigo: Editorial Galaxia, 2006 (pp. 14 and 219–222).

Capitaine, Simone. *Moi, Un cobaye.* Paris: SEFA, 1975.

Carrete Rivera, Manoel. *Máis que nós, ninguén.* Barcelona: Centro Galego de Barcelona, 2008 (pp. 165–168).

Cartier, Clément. *Les grandes affaires criminelles de l'Aude.* Toulouse: Éditions Privat, 1996.

Catalá, Neus. *De la Resistencia y la deportación.* Barcelona: Adgena, 1984 (pp. 86 and 206).

Centelles, Agustí. *Diario de un fotógrafo, Bram 1939.* Barcelona: Ediciones Península, 2009.

Chacón, Dulce. *La voz dormida.* Madrid: Editorial Alfaguara, 2002.

Château, Gilbert. *L'enfer de Ravensbrück.* Paris: Éditions Rouff, 1949.

Cuevas, Tomasa. *Cárcel de mujeres (1939–1945).* Barcelona: Sirocco Books, 1995.

Cuevas, Tomasa. *Testimonios de mujeres en las cárceles franquistas.* Huesca: Instituto de Estudios Aragoneses, 2004.

Delpard, Raphaël. *Les convois de la honte. Enquête sur la SNCF et la déportation.* Neuilly-sur-Seine: Michel Lafon, 2005.

Domingo, Carmen. *Histoire politique des femmes espagnoles de la IIe République à la fin du franquisme.* Rennes: Presses Universitaires de Rennes, 2008 (pp. 183, 189, 193 and 296).

Doña, Juana. *Desde la noche y la niebla (mujeres en las cárceles franquistas).* Madrid: Ediciones de la Torre, 1978.

Doña, Juana. *Querido Eugenio.* Barcelona: Editorial Lumen, 2003.

Ducher, Guillaume. *Les camps tragiques,* Revue «Lectures pour tous». Paris: Hachette, 1934; Paris: Cartouche, 2005.

Dufournier, Denise. *La maison des mortes.* Paris: Librairie Hachette, 1945.

F.A.C.E.E.F. *Memorias del olvido.* Paris: Instituto Cervantes, 1996 (pp. 140 and 163).

FIM. *Presas de Franco.* Madrid: Fundación de Investigaciones Marxistas, 2007.

Fondation des Mémoriaux de Buchenwald et Mitelbau-Dora, *Les femmes oubliées de Buchenwald.* Paris: Éditions Nicolas Chaudun, 2005.

Fonseca, Carlos. *Trece rosas rojas.* Madrid: Temas de Hoy, 2004.

García, Consuelo. *Las cárceles de Soledad Real.* Madrid: Editorial Alfaguara, 1982.

García-Madrid, Ángeles. *Réquiem por la libertad.* Madrid: Editorial Alianza Hispánica, 1982.

González Álvarez, Mónica. *Guardianas nazis. El lado femenino del mal.* Madrid: Editorial Edaf, 2012 (pp. 209–213).

Gran Enciclopedia Gallega. Santiago de Compostela: Cañada Editor, 1974 (Vol. 22, p. 254).

Gros-Duruisseau, Andrée, and Annie Marais. *Le cahier*. La Couronne: CDPP de la Charente, 2008.

Guérin, Alain. *Chronique de la Résistance*. Paris: Omnibus, 2000.

Hernández Holgado, Fernando. *Mujeres encarceladas en la prisión de Ventas: de la República al franquismo, 1931–1941*. Madrid: Marcial Pons Editores, 2003 (pp. 29–31, 118, 163, 164, 207, 221–223, 258, 259, 355–358).

Hernández Holgado, Fernando. *Soledad Real*. Madrid: Ediciones del Horto, 2001.

Karay, Felicja. *Hasag-Leipzig Slave Labour Camp for Women*. London: Valentine Mitchell, 2002.

Krause-Schmitt, Ursula, and Christine Krause. *Avec les yeux des survivants. Un parcours dans le mémorial de Ravensbrück*. Stuttgart: Lagergemeinschaft Ravensbrück Freundeskreiss, 2003.

Langhoff, W. *Les soldats du marais. Sous la schlague des nazis*. Paris: Librairie Plon, 1935.

L'herminier, Jeannette, and Germaine Tillion. *Les robes grises*. Strasbourg: Bibliothèque Nationale et Universitaire, 2011.

London, Lise. *La mégère de la rue Daguerre*. Paris: Éditions du Seuil, 1995.

Llor, Montserrat. *Vivos en el averno nazi*. Barcelona: Ed. Crítica (Planeta), 2014 (p. 311).

Mangini, Shirley. *Recuerdos de la Resistencia. La voz de las mujeres de la Guerra Civil Española*. Barcelona: Ediciones Península, 1997 (pp. 127, 134, 140–143 and 148).

Marco, Aurora. *Diccionario de mulleres galegas*. Santiago de Compostela: Xunta de Galicia, 2007 (pp. 305–307).

Maury, Lucien. *La Résistance audoise*. Comité d'Histoire de la Résistance du Département de l'Aude, 1980 (Vol. II , pp. 176 and 183).

Memorial da Liberdade, represión e resistencia en Galiza 1936–1977. Santiago de Compostela: Xunta de Galicia, 2007 (pp. 385–388, 390, 391 and 423).

Mínguez Anaya, Adrián Blas. *El campo de Bram*. Valencia: Edición Memoria Viva, 2009.

Moine, André. *La déportation et la résistance en Afrique du Nord (1939–1945)*. Paris: Éditions Sociales, 1972.

Molinero C., M. Sala, and J. Sobrequés. *Una inmensa prisión*. Barcelona: Ed. Crítica, 2003 (pp. 203, 235, 238 and 246).

Morisse, Jeanine. *Là, d'où je viens*. Portet-sur-Garonne: Éditions Empreinte, 2007.

Morrison, Jack G. *Ravensbrück: Everyday Life a Women's Concentration Camp 1939–45*. Princeton, NJ: Markus Wiener Publishers, 2000.

Núñez Díaz-Balart, Mirta, and Antonio Rojas Friend, Consejo de Guerra. *Los fusilamientos en el Madrid de la posguerra (1939–1945)*. Madrid: Compañía Literaria, 1997 (pp. 43, 44, 49, 67 and 68).

Ouzoulias, Albert, 'colonel André'. *Les bataillons de la jeunesse*. Paris: Éditions Sociales, 1967.

Piquee-Audrain, Daniel and Petit, Maurice. *Plus jamais ça! Dessins du camp de Mauthausen*. Paris: Imprimerie Petit et Rousseau, 1964.

Pons Prades, Eduardo. *El holocausto de los republicanos españoles*. Barcelona: Belacqva de Ediciones, 2005 (pp. 122–126).

Pons Prades, Eduardo. *Republicanos españoles en la segunda guerra mundial*. Barcelona: Editorial Planeta, 1975 (pp. 97 and 103).

Pons Prades, Eduardo, and Mariano Constante. *Los cerdos del comandante. Españoles en los campos de exterminio nazis*. Barcelona: Librería Editorial Argos, 1978 (pp. 111–115).

Portella Coll, Josep. *Miquel Amantegui*. Menorca: Llibre d'Exilis, 2012.

Rafaneau-Boj, Marie-Claude. *Los campos de concentración de los refugiados españoles en Francia (1939–1945)*. Barcelona: Ediciones Omega, 1995 (p. 328).

Reich, Ernst. *Héritage vivant*. Dresden: Éditions Zeit im Bild, 1968.

Résistance et clandestinité dans l'Aude. Carcassonne: Archives Départementales de l'Aude, 2010.

Riveiro Coello, Antón. *Laura no deserto*. Vigo: Editorial Galaxia, 2011.

Roig, Montserrat. *Els catalans als camps nazis*. Barcelona: Edicions 62, 1977 (pp. 104, 512, 533 and 534).

Roig, Montserrat. *Noche y Niebla. Los catalanes en los campos nazis*. Barcelona: Edicions 62, 1978 (pp. 302 and 321).

Rolland, Eduardo. *Galicia en guerra*. Vigo: Edicións Xerais, 2006 (pp. 98–101).

Rougier-Lecoq, Violette. *Témoignages, 36 dessins à la plume. Ravensbrück*. Paris: Les Deux Sirènes, 1948.

Roux, Catherine. *Triangle rouge*. Paris: Éditions France-Empire, 1968.

Ruby, Marcel. *Le livre de la déportation*. Paris: Éditions Robert Laffont, 1995.

Saint-Clair, Simone. *Ravensbrück: L'Enfer des femmes*. Paris: Éditions Julles Tallandier, 1946.

Santidrían, Víctor Manuel. *Historia do PCE en Galicia (1920–1968)*. Ares: Edicións do Castro, 2002 (p. 604).

Sanz, Miguel Ángel. *Luchando en tierras de Francia*. Madrid: Ediciones de la Torre, 1981 (pp. 180 and 184).

Sigaud, Dominique. *Le piège des loups: Les 175 maisons de la Gestapo en France*. Paris: Éditions Stock, 2012 (p. 293).

Solé, Felip, and Grégory Tuban. *Camp d'Argelers 1939–1942*. Barcelona: Cossetanià Edicions, 2011.

Strebel, Bernhard. *Ravensbrück, un complexe concentrationnaire*. Paris: Éditions Fayard, 2005.

Thomas, Rémi. *Bordeaux Ravensbrück Leipzig Bordeaux*. Paris: Le Manuscrit, 2006.

Tillion, Germaine. *Ravensbrück*. Paris: Éditions du Seuil, 1973.

Tillion, Germaine. *Une opérette à Ravensbrück*. Paris: Éditions Point, 2007.

Torán, Rosa. *Los campos de concentración nazis, palabras contra el olvido*. Barcelona: Ediciones Península, 2005 (pp. 165–166).

Torres Rondón, Elba. *Crónicas de la emigración, 20 mujeres y una leyenda*. Vigo: Grupo de Comunicación de Galicia en el mundo, 2010 (pp. 215–222).

Toulouse-Lautrec, Béatrix. *J'ai eu vingt ans à Ravensbrück*. Paris: Perrin, 1991.

Triay-Pascuchi, Miguel. *Sable amer*. Carcassonne: ed. F.R.E. 39, 2008 (p. 230).

Vv. Aa. *Contra Franco. Testimonios y reflexiones*. Madrid: Ed. Vosa & Cedall, 2006 (p. 212).

Vv. Aa. *Les femmes dans la Résistance en France*. Paris: Éditions Tallandier, 2003.

Vv. Aa. *Memorial de las españolas deportadas a Ravensbrück*. Barcelona: Amics de Ravensbrück, 2012 (pp. 102–108 and 159).

Vv. Aa. *Ravensbrück (Cahiers du Rhône n° 20)*. Neuchâtel: Éditions de la Baconnière, 1946.

Yusta Rodrigo, Mercedes. *Madres coraje contra Franco: La Unión de Mujeres Españolas en Francia del antifascismo a la Guerra Fría (1941–1950)*. Madrid: Ediciones Cátedra, 2009 (p. 202).

Index

The Pluto Press Newsletter

Hello friend of Pluto!

Want to stay on top of the best radical books
we publish?

Then sign up to be the first to hear about our
new books, as well as special events,
podcasts and videos.

You'll also get 50% off your first order with us
when you sign up.

Come and join us!

Go to bit.ly/PlutoNewsletter

Thanks to our Patreon subscriber:

Ciaran Kane

Who has shown generosity and comradeship in support of our publishing.